T0210695

Cross-Language
Information Retrieval

Synthesis Lectures in Human Language Technologies

Editor

Graeme Hirst, University of Toronto

Synthesis Lectures on Human Language Technologies publishes monographs on topics relating to natural language processing, computational linguistics, information retrieval, and spoken language understanding. Emphasis is placed on important new techniques, on new applications, and on topics that combine two or more HLT subfields.

Cross-Language Information Retrieval
Jian-Yun Nie
2010

Data-Intensive Text Processing with MapReduce
Jimmy Lin, Chris Dyer
2010

Semantic Role Labeling
Martha Palmer, Daniel Gildea, Nianwen Xue
2010

Spoken Dialogue Systems
Kristiina Jokinen, Michael McTear
2010

Introduction to Chinese Natural Language Processing
Kam-Fai Wong, Wenji Li, Ruifeng Xu, Zheng-sheng Zhang
2009

Introduction to Linguistic Annotation and Text Analytics
Graham Wilcock
2009

Dependency Parsing
Sandra Kübler, Ryan McDonald, Joakim Nivre
2009

Statistical Language Models for Information Retrieval
ChengXiang Zhai
2008

© Springer Nature Switzerland AG 2022

Reprint of original edition © Morgan & Claypool 2010

All rights reserved. No part of this publication may be reproduced, stored in a retrieval system, or transmitted in any form or by any means—electronic, mechanical, photocopy, recording, or any other except for brief quotations in printed reviews, without the prior permission of the publisher.

Cross-Language Information Retrieval
Jian-Yun Nie

ISBN: 978-3-031-01010-1   paperback

ISBN: 978-3-031-02138-1   ebook

DOI: 10.1007/978-3-031-02138-1

A Publication in the Springer series

SYNTHESIS LECTURES IN HUMAN LANGUAGE TECHNOLOGIES

Lecture #8

Series Editor: Graeme Hirst, University of Toronto

Series ISSN

ISSN 1947-4040 print

ISSN 1947-4059 electronic

Cross-Language Information Retrieval

Jian-Yun Nie
University of Montreal

SYNTHESIS LECTURES IN HUMAN LANGUAGE TECHNOLOGIES #8

ABSTRACT

Search for information is no longer exclusively limited within the native language of the user, but is more and more extended to other languages. This gives rise to the problem of cross-language information retrieval (CLIR), whose goal is to find relevant information written in a different language to a query. In addition to the problems of monolingual information retrieval (IR), translation is the key problem in CLIR: one should translate either the query or the documents from a language to another. However, this translation problem is not identical to full-text machine translation (MT): the goal is not to produce a human-readable translation, but a translation suitable for finding relevant documents. Specific translation methods are thus required.

The goal of this book is to provide a comprehensive description of the specific problems arising in CLIR, the solutions proposed in this area, as well as the remaining problems. The book starts with a general description of the monolingual IR and CLIR problems. Different classes of approaches to translation are then presented: approaches using an MT system, dictionary-based translation and approaches based on parallel and comparable corpora. In addition, the typical retrieval effectiveness using different approaches is compared. It will be shown that translation approaches specifically designed for CLIR can rival and outperform high-quality MT systems. Finally, the book offers a look into the future that draws a strong parallel between query expansion in monolingual IR and query translation in CLIR, suggesting that many approaches developed in monolingual IR can be adapted to CLIR.

The book can be used as an introduction to CLIR. Advanced readers can also find more technical details and discussions about the remaining research challenges in the future. It is suitable to new researchers who intend to carry out research on CLIR.

KEYWORDS

cross-language information retrieval; multilingual information retrieval; query translation; document translation; translation model; machine translation / statistical machine translation; dictionary-based translation; parallel corpus; comparable corpus; query expansion; transliteration; mining of translation relations / resources

Dedication

To my dear son Guillaume (子吟).

Contents

Preface xiii

1. Introduction 1
   1.1 General IR Problems 1
   1.2 General IR Approaches 2
       1.2.1 IR Models 3
           1.2.1.1 Boolean Models 3
           1.2.1.2 Vector Space Model 4
           1.2.1.3 Probabilistic Models 5
           1.2.1.4 Statistical Language Models 6
       1.2.2 Query Expansion 8
       1.2.3 System Evaluation 10
   1.3 Language Problems in IR 12
       1.3.1 European Languages 12
           1.3.1.1 Word Stemming 12
           1.3.1.2 Decompounding 12
       1.3.2 East Asian Languages 14
           1.3.2.1 Chinese and Word Segmentation 14
           1.3.2.2 Japanese and Korean 17
       1.3.3 Other Languages 17
   1.4 The Problems of Cross-Language Information Retrieval 18
       1.4.1 Query Translation vs. Document Translation 19
       1.4.2 Using Pivot Language and Interlingua 20
   1.5 Approaches to Translation in CLIR 21
   1.6 The Need for Cross-Language and Multilingual IR 23
   1.7 The History of CLIR 24

Preface

Searching for information is part of our daily life in this information era. Ideally, we are interested in information written in our native language. However, relevant information is not always available in our native language, and we are also interested in finding information written in other languages in many situations. This gives rise to the problem of cross-language information retrieval (CLIR), whose goal is to find relevant information written in a different language to a query. In addition to the problems of monoligual Information Retrieval (IR), translation is the key problem in CLIR. The goal of this book is to provide a comprehensive description of the specific problems that have arisen in CLIR, the solutions proposed in this area, as well as the remaining problems.

The book is organized into the following chapters:

Chapter 1 contains a general description of the IR and CLIR problems. We first provide a description of general IR problems and the approaches proposed in monolingual IR. This description provides the necessary background knowledge on IR for readers who are not familiar with IR. Specific problems to CLIR are then introduced. We will discuss the general strategies that we can use to solve these problems. Readers familiar with IR and CLIR problems can skip this chapter or some sections of this chapter.

Chapter 2 focuses on a family of approaches based on manually constructed translation resources and tools. Namely, we will describe the general approaches to machine translation (MT) as well as their suitability to CLIR. Approaches based on bilingual dictionaries will be presented as possible alternatives.

In Chapter 3, we describe approaches exploiting parallel and comparable texts. We also describe attempts to mine translation resources automatically from the Web.

Chapter 4 describes some approaches to further improve CLIR effectiveness.

Finally, in Chapter 5, we provide a view of CLIR for future developments based on the parallel between query expansion in monolingual IR and query translation in CLIR and propose that query translation can inspire much from query expansion. An example is given to illustrate it.

Acknowledgement

A large part of this book is based on the author's work with his graduate students and collaborators. Without the contributions from the students and collaborators, it would be impossible for him to write this book. The author would like to thank his students Jing Bai, Guihong Cao, Jiang Chen, Lixin Shi, and Michel Simard and his collaborators, in particular, Jianfeng Gao and Wessel Kraaij, for their great work.

CHAPTER 1

Introduction

Searching for information is a part of our everyday life, be it for leisure or professional activities. In most cases, people want to retrieve relevant information written in their native language, usually the language of the query. However, we are more and more exposed to information written in other languages. The World-Wide Web provides a wealth of rich information in different media and languages which people want to access. There are increasing needs to search for information in languages different from that of the query. For example, one may want to retrieve documents written in French or Chinese with a query written in English. This gives rise to the problem of cross-language information retrieval (CLIR), whose aim is to retrieve information in a language different from the language of the query.

This book is concerned with the problems of CLIR. Through different chapters, we will discuss about the problems that have arisen in CLIR as well as the possible solutions to deal with them.

1.1 GENERAL IR PROBLEMS

To better situate the problems, let us start with a brief description of the general Information Retrieval (IR) problems. This allows us to introduce the particular CLIR problems later.

Information retrieval is concerned with the problem of finding *relevant information*, or relevant documents containing such information, for a particular *information need*, from a large set of documents (e.g., a large database of documents or the Web). For example, a user may want to find information about a product (e.g., the size of memory of iPod) from the Web. A document is relevant if it contains such information. What makes this problem particularly difficult is the fact that pieces of information are not directly accessible and manipulable. What we access and manipulate is a *description* of it. Such a description is not unique. The same piece of information, say "there is a major earthquake in China in 2008," can be described in various forms in a document: in different media (text, image, video, speech, etc.) and in different (either natural or formal) languages. In a similar way, the information need of the user can also be specified in various ways. For example, a user who wants to identify the above piece of information may specify the need by the queries "earthquake in China" or "recent natural disaster in China." A good IR system should be able to identify the above piece of information for it. This example describes what is desired by users: to retrieve relevant documents whatever the form in which the information is described. Indeed, when a human being judges if a document is relevant (i.e., contains the relevant information) for an information need, he/she judges according to the semantic contents of the document rather than its form (in most cases). This means that a semantic interpretation of the document contents is made when relevance judgment is made. Ideally, an IR system, whose aim is to satisfy the user in their information seeking process, should also make a similar semantic interpretation so as to arrive at a relevant judgment similar to that of the user. Unfortunately, such a semantic interpretation is (so far) impossible for computers. The current state of the art of IR still strongly relies on simple information representations (e.g., using a set of keywords) without deep interpretation.

The above situation occurs in general textual information retrieval or search engines when an information need and the pieces of information looked for are described in natural languages. Descriptions in natural language are not directly comparable and manipulable by a computer. To enable this, a natural language description has to be represented in some internal representation form to be searchable. The core problems in IR are intimately related to that of representation of pieces of information and to the matching between the representations. These problems are dealt with in IR models, which we will describe briefly in the next section.

1.2   GENERAL IR APPROACHES

The general approach to IR can be illustrated by Figure 1.1. In general, an IR system is constructed to work on a specific *document collection*, which could be a digital library, a set of specialized documents in an area (e.g., Medline) or the whole World-Wide Web.

A user who desires to find some information in the document collection should describe his/her *information need* in a *query*. A query can be a long sentence or even an example document

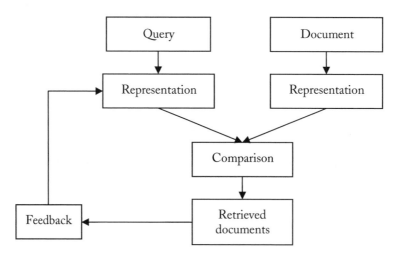

FIGURE 1.1: Typical processes of IR systems.

in some cases, but it is usually very short containing a few words. On the Web, typical queries are formed by 2–3 words. On both the query and the document, similar processes of *indexing* are carried out in order to "understand," to some extent, what the user desires to find and what the document talks about. In many cases, these processes mainly involve the extraction of important keywords that represent the main contents of them and to weigh them appropriately. This results in an internal representation for each document and query.

Given a query representation and a document representation, a *relevance score* is determined for each document according to how strongly the document representation corresponds to that of the query. This score intends to reflect the degree of relevance of the document to the user's information need. Optionally, a *feedback* process can take place once a list of documents is identified by the system. True *relevance feedback* relies on the relevance judgments by the user on some of the retrieved documents: a list of retrieved documents is presented to the user and the user is asked to judge the relevance of some of them. According to the indication of the document's relevance by the user, the system can create a new, hopefully better, query representation, and the retrieval process is repeated using the new query. In practice, however, the user is often unwilling to provide relevance judgments. So a *pseudo-relevance feedback* (PRF) can be performed by assuming the top retrieved documents to be relevant.

What distinguishes the most an IR approach from another is the retrieval *model* that it uses. IR models define the core elements of an IR approach. To better understand how IR systems operate, let us describe briefly some commonly used IR models in the next section.

1.2.1 IR Models

The role of an IR model is to define the internal representation of documents and queries as well as the score function. Many IR models have been proposed and used in IR. In this section, we will only describe the most commonly used ones: Boolean model, vector space model, probabilistic model, and language model. Interested readers can find even more detailed descriptions and discussions in Salton and McGill (1983), Baeza-Yates and Ribeiro-Neto (1999), Manning et al. (2008), and Zhai (2009).

Most models are built upon the notion of *term*. In IR, a term refers to a basic unit used in the representation. It can be a word (e.g., "computer"), a word stem (e.g., "comput"), or a phrase (e.g., "computer system"), depending on the indexing process used. A term is intended to represent a basic semantic unit of the content. More complex representations are constructed by combining terms in different ways. We will see several ways to determine such terms in different languages in Section 1.3. In the meantime, let us assume that a set of terms have been identified.

1.2.1.1 Boolean Models

In Boolean models, documents are represented by a conjunction of terms, such as $D = t_1 \wedge t_2 \wedge t_3$, which means that the terms t_1, t_2, and t_3 are present in the document D. Equivalently, this document can also be represented by a set of terms: $D = \{t_1, t_2, t_3\}$. Terms not in the Boolean expression are assumed to be absent. A query is represented by a Boolean expression of terms such as $Q = (t_1 \wedge t_2) \vee t_3$. A document is considered as relevant if and only if we have the logical implication $D \rightarrow Q$. For example, the document representation given above can logically imply the query expression, i.e., we have $D \rightarrow Q$. Therefore, the document is retrieved for the query.

One can notice that no term weighting is involved in this simple model. Term weighting has been integrated into extended Boolean models so that a document is represented by a set of weighted terms. Consequently, the logical implication $D \rightarrow Q$ can also be weighted, for example, by using a fuzzy set extesion of the Boolean logic (Radecki, 1979) (Kraft and Buell, 1983), p-norm (Salton et al. 1983), or other more heuristic extensions.

1.2.1.2 Vector Space Model

The vector space model (VSM) (Salton and McGill, 1983; Salton et al., 1975) uses a vector to represent a document or a query. The vector space is formed by all the terms the system recognizes in the documents. In the document vector and the query vector, each element (d_i or q_i, $1 \leq i \leq n$) represents the weight of the corresponding term in the document or the query.

$$
\begin{array}{ll}
\text{vector space:} & \langle\, t_1 \quad t_2 \quad t_3 \quad \ldots \quad t_n \,\rangle \\
\text{document:} & \langle\, d_1 \quad d_2 \quad d_3 \quad \ldots \quad d_n \,\rangle \\
\text{query:} & \langle\, q_1 \quad q_2 \quad q_3 \quad \ldots \quad q_n \,\rangle
\end{array}
$$

The weights d_i or q_i could be binary, i.e., 1 representing the presence, or 0 representing the absence, of a term in the document or the query. However, the most commonly used method is the tf*idf weighting schema. tf means *term frequency* within the document (or the query), and idf means *inverse document frequency*, which is usually calculated as follows:

$$
idf(t_i) = \log \frac{N}{n(t_i)}
$$

where t_i is a term in the vocabulary, N is the number of documents in the whole document collection and $n(t_i)$ is the number of documents containing t_i (also called document frequency). The general idea behind tf*idf weighting is that, the more a term appears in a document (or a query), the more it is important (the tf factor); the less the term is common among all the documents in the collection, the more it is specific, thus important (the idf factor).

Given the above vector representations, the score of relevance is estimated by a similarity between the vectors. The most commonly used similarity is called *cosine similarity*, defined as follows:

$$
sim(\bar{D}, \bar{Q}) = \frac{\bar{D} \bullet \bar{Q}}{|\bar{D}| \times |\bar{Q}|}
$$

where $|\bar{D}|$ is the length of the vector, defined as $|\bar{D}| = \sqrt{\sum_{i=1}^{n}(d_i)^2}$ ($|\bar{Q}|$ is defined analogically) and $\bar{D} \bullet \bar{Q}$ is the dot product.

1.2.1.3 Probabilistic Models

In probabilistic model, the relevance score of a document D to a query Q is estimated according to $P(rel|D, Q)$, where *rel* means "relevance."

The simplest probabilistic model is the binary independence retrieval (BIR) model (Robertson and Spärck Jones, 1976). The BIR model assumes that terms are independent. Documents are sorted according to the log-odd between $P(rel|D, Q)$ and $P(irrel|D,Q)$ (where *irrel* denotes irrelevance), i.e.:

$$Score(Q,D) = \log \frac{P(rel|D,Q)}{P(irrel|D,Q)} = \log \frac{P(D|Q,rel)P(rel|Q)}{P(D|Q,irrel)P(irrel|Q)}$$

$$\propto \log \frac{P(D|Q,rel)}{P(D|Q,irrel)}$$

A document D is represented as a set of independent binary events $\{x_1, \ldots, x_n\}$, where $x_i=1$ and $x_i = 0$ represent respectively the presence and absence of term t_i in the document. So, we have:

$$Score(Q,D) \propto \sum_{x_i \in D} \log \frac{P(x_i=1|Q,rel)^{x_i}(1-P(x_i=1|Q,rel))^{1-x_i}}{P(x_i=1|Q,irrel)^{x_i}(1-P(x_i=1|Q,irrel))^{1-x_i}}$$

$$= \sum_{x_i \in D} x_i \log \frac{P(x_i=1|Q,rel)(1-P(x_i=1|Q,irrel))}{P(x_i=1|Q,irrel)(1-P(x_i=1|Q,rel))} + Const$$

where *Const* is a constant independent of the document, and can be ignored for document reranking.

The key problem is the estimation of the conditional probabilities $P(x_i=1|Q,rel)$ and $P(x_i=1|Q,irrel)$. Ideally, we would require a set of sample documents whose relevance is judged. Given such sets of sample documents, we can build the following contingency table for each term t_i (where N is the total number of samples judged, R the number of relevant samples, r_i the number of relevant samples containing t_i and n_i the number of samples containing t_i):

TABLE 1.1: Contingency table of term occurrences.

	RELEVANT	IRRELEVANT	TOTAL
#Doc Containing t	r_i	$n_i - r_i$	n_i
#Doc not containing t	$R - r_i$	$N - n_i - (R - r_i)$	$N - n_i$
#Total Doc	R	$N - R$	N

With the information given in the table 1.1, we estimate the probabilities as follows:

$$p(x_i = 1 | Q, rel) = \frac{r_i}{R} \text{ and } p(x_i = 1 | Q, irrel) = \frac{n_i - r_i}{N - R}$$

we then have:

$$Score(Q, D) \propto \sum_{x_i \in D} x_i \log \frac{r_i(N - n_i - R + r_i)}{(R - r_i)(n_i - r_i)}$$

$$= \sum_{(x_i = 1) \in D} \log \frac{r_i(N - n_i - R + r_i)}{(R - r_i)(n_i - r_i)}$$

In this formula, we can view $\log \frac{r_i(N - n_i - R + r_i)}{(R - r_i)(n_i - r_i)}$ as the weight of the term t_i present in D. Documents is thus ranked according to the sum of weights of all the terms it contains. To deal with the cases with zero occurrences in the contingency table, Robertson and Spärck Jones proposed the following slightly smoothed weighting: $\log \frac{(r_i + 0.5)(N - n_i - R + r_i + 0.5)}{(R - r_i + 0.5)(n_i - r_i + 0.5)}$.

In practice, usually no relevant and irrelevant documents can be provided in advance. In such a situation, several methods are used to approximate the conditional probabilities (Baeza-Yates and Ribeiro-Neto 1999). For example, one can assume that the number of relevant documents in a document collection is very small compared to the number of irrelevant document. Therefore, $P(x_i = 1 | Q, irrel)$ can be approximated by $\frac{n_i}{N}$, where N is the total number of documents in the collection and n_i the number of documents containing t_i. It can also be assumed that a term has an equal probability to be present or absent in a relevant document. So, $P(x_i = 1 | Q, rel) = 0.5$.

More sophisticated models than BIR have been proposed in the literature. For example, van Rijsbergen (1979) proposed a model to consider the inter-dependency between terms. Fuhr (1992) proposed several other probabilistic models for IR. However, the description of these models is beyond the scope of this book.

1.2.1.4 Statistical Language Models
Statistical language models are originally proposed to model general languages in speech recognition and machine translation (Brown et al., 1993; Jelinek, 1998; Gao et al., 2002). Ponte and Croft (1998) are the first ones to use them in IR. This approach is followed by many other researchers (Hiemstra and Kraaij, 1998; Miller et al., 1999; Berger and Lafferty, 1999; Song and Croft, 1999; Zhai and Lafferty, 2001a; Zhai and Lafferty, 2001b; Bai et al., 2005). The general idea is to use

$P(D|Q)$ to estimate the score of relevance of the document D to the query Q. Using Bayes rule, we have:

$$P(D|Q) = \frac{P(Q|D)P(D)}{P(Q)} \propto P(Q|D)P(D)$$

The probability $P(Q)$ in the above equation is ignored because it is document-independent, thus will not affect the ranking of documents. Furthermore, in most studies, $P(D)$ is assumed to be uniform for simplification (however, it is possible to assign different probabilities to documents, e.g., by using PageRank score (Brin and Page, 1998)). We then arrive at a ranking function based on $P(Q|D)$, which is often called generative model.

The query Q is usually considered as a set of independent terms, i.e., $Q = \{t_1, t_2, ...\}$. We then have:

$$P(Q|D) = \prod_{t_i \in Q} P(t_i|D)$$

The probability $P(t_i|D)$ is estimated by a statistical language model (usually word unigram model) of the document. Let us denote the language model by θ_D. Using log-likelihood as the document score, we have:

$$\text{score}(D,Q) = \log P(Q|\theta_D) = \sum_{t_i \in Q} \log P(t_i|\theta_D)$$

The key problem is the estimation of the language model θ_D. The simplest method is by maximum likelihood (ML), i.e.:

$$P_{\text{ML}}(t_i|\theta_D) = \frac{f(t_i, D)}{|D|}$$

However, this simple way may not work for IR because if any query term is unseen in a document, the probability $P(Q|\theta_D)$ becomes 0. This is often a too strict condition for IR—in many cases, even if a document contains part of the query terms, the document can still be relevant. One only has to think about the case where the document contains synonyms or related terms to the missing query terms. To solve this problem, smoothing is used. The goal of smoothing is to avoid the above zero-probability problem. A more fundamental principle behind the general smoothing principle is that a text (or a set of texts) we use to model a language only covers a limited number of linguistic phenomena (term in our case) in the language. Other phenomena may be unseen from the text, yet they are fully legitimate in the language. To cope with the partial coverage of the training text, we would rather render the observation less absolute—those that are not observed in the text can still have a certain probability to occur. So, smoothing tries to assign some (small) probabilities to the terms that do not appear in the training text (document, in our case).

Two common smoothing methods are used in IR (Zhai and Lafferty, 2001b): Jalinek–Mercer smoothing:

$$P(t_i \mid \theta_D) = \lambda P_{ML}(t_i \mid \theta_D) + (1 - \lambda) P_{ML}(t_i \mid \theta_C)$$

Dirichlet smoothing:

$$P(t_i \mid \theta_D) = \frac{f(t_i, D) + \mu P_{ML}(t_i \mid \theta_C)}{|D| + \mu}$$

where θ_C is the language model estimated for the whole document collection (called collection model) and $\lambda \in [0,1]$ and μ (Dirichlet prior) are smoothing parameters.

For a detailed study on smoothing methods for IR, readers can refer to Zhai and Lafferty (2001b) and Zhai (2009).

In addition to the above generative model, a discriminative model is also proposed, which is based on cross-entropy or the Kullback–Leibler divergence (KL-divergence):

$$\text{score}(D, Q) = \sum_{t_i \in V} P(t_i \mid \theta_Q) \log P(t_i \mid \theta_D)$$

$$\propto \sum_{t_i \in V} P(t_i \mid \theta_Q) \log \frac{P(t_i \mid \theta_D)}{P(t_i \mid \theta_Q)} = - KL(\theta_Q \| \theta_D)$$

where V is the vocabulary. In many cases, the query model $P(t_i \mid \theta_Q)$ is estimated using simple maximum likelihood estimation, but the document model is smoothed.

1.2.2 Query Expansion

The basic IR models we just described rely on the initial query provided by the user. It is known that the initial query of the user is not always the best description of the intended information need. For example, the user may choose to use a term that is not usually used in the relevant documents, or the query may specify only part of the information need. For example, a user who intends to find information about "the problems of deforestation in Amazon" may issues queries such as "Amazon forest destruction" (using related terms) or "Amazon forest" (partial specification). All these queries can only identify part of the relevant documents, while also retrieving irrelevant documents.

To solve this problem, i.e., to create a better query representation, query expansion is often proposed as a solution. Query expansion aims at enriching or expanding the initial query in such a way that the expanded query can better match the intended documents. The common method consists of adding a set of related terms into the query so as to enlarge the coverage of the query. In doing so, one may expect that the new query can cover more relevant documents, which enhance the recall measure (see Section 1.2.3).

There are two main issues in query expansion: (1) the selection of expansion terms and (2) the way that the expansion terms are weighted and added in the query.

To determine related expansion terms, three families of methods can be used:

(1) An external lexical database such as a thesaurus (e.g., Wordnet (Miller, 1995)) can be used to suggest related terms. For example, for each term (e.g., "computer"), Wordnet contains its synonyms (e.g., "information processing system"), hypernyms (e.g., "machine"), hyponyms (e.g., "digital computer"), and so on. One can choose to use some types of relation and consider the related terms as expansion terms. For example, one can choose to use synonyms and hypernyms. So, "information processing system" and "machine" will be used as expansion terms. The use of Wordnet has been investigated in Voorhees (1993) and Voorhees (1994). Unfortunately, the experiments using such a resource have not shown to be effective: no or little gain in retrieval effectiveness has been observed. Some of the problems relating to this method are as follows:

1. The resource used may have a limited coverage of the terms we encounter in queries, leading to unbalanced expansion on some of the terms only.
2. Such resources are often built for purposes other than IR. Terms that appear to be strongly related (e.g., between "computer" and "machine") could rather bring in noise when added into the query.
3. Finally, there are many ambiguities that cannot be solved. For example, "computer" has two meanings in Wordnet: a machine or a human estimator. As no effective means exists to determine the correct meaning of such a term in a query, it is expanded in all the senses, which will introduce additional noise into the retrieval results.

(2) One can also use a less precise but more robust analysis of co-occurrences to construct a statistical similarity thesaurus automatically (Qiu and Frei, 1993; Crouch and Yang, 1992). The assumption used is: the more two terms co-occur in texts, the more they are related. Various measures have been defined based on term co-occurrences, for example, $sim(t_1, t_2) = \dfrac{co(t_1, t_2)}{\max(f(t_1), f(t_2))}$, where $co(t_1, t_2)$ is the frequency of co-occurrences of two terms and $f(t_1)$ and $f(t_2)$ the frequency of occurrences of each term. Query expansion based on co-occurrence analysis is commonly used in IR and turned out to be quite effective (Xu and Croft, 1996).

(3) A third approach is based on pseudo-relevance feedback: a set of terms are extracted from the top retrieved documents using the initial query. These terms can be the most frequent ones in these documents, the ones that are the most distinctive compared to the whole collection (Zhai and Lafferty, 2001a) or the ones that co-occur with the query terms within some contexts (e.g., text windows).

The second and the third approaches are in fact related. One may think of the third approach as a special kind of co-occurrence analysis, but within the subset of documents at the top retrieval results. Xu and Croft (1996) call the second and third approaches, respectively, global and local context analyses. It is found that local context analysis (using top-retrieved documents) is more effective than global context analysis (using the whole collection). The main reason is that, as local context analysis is performed only on documents more related to the query, it generates less noise than global context analysis.

Once a set of expansion terms is identified, the second issue in query expansion is the way to weight and add expansion terms into the query. This depends on the retrieval model used.

In vector space model, one usually uses the Rocchio formula to construct a new query vector $\bar{Q}'$ as follows:

$$\bar{Q}' = \alpha \bar{Q} + (1-\alpha)\bar{E}$$

where $\bar{Q}$ is the original query vector, $\bar{E}$ is the vector formed by the selected expansion terms, and α ($\in [0,1]$) a parameter fixed manually.

In language modeling approaches, a new query model θ_E can be estimated from the set of top-retrieved documents (Zhai and Lafferty, 2001a), and then combined with the original query model θ_Q in a similar way:

$$P(t_i|\theta_{Q'}) = \alpha P(t_i|\theta_Q) + (1-\alpha)P(t_i|\theta_E) .$$

Pseudo-relevance feedback documents are exploited in a different way to estimate the query model in Relevance model (Lavrenko and Croft, 2001): feedback documents are viewed as samples of relevant documents, from which a relevance model θ_R for the given query is derived and then used to rank documents.

1.2.3   System Evaluation

The effectiveness of IR systems can be evaluated by several measures. The basic measures are *precision* and *recall*. *Precision* is the fraction of the retrieved documents which are relevant, i.e.,

$$\text{Precision} = \frac{\#\ \text{retrieved relevant documents}}{\#\ \text{retrieved documents}}$$

Recall is the fraction of the relevant documents which have been retrieved, i.e.,

$$\text{Recall} = \frac{\#\ \text{retrieved relevant documents}}{\#\ \text{relevant documents in the collection}}$$

There is a trade-off between precision and recall: when precision increases, recall usually decreases, and vice versa. To measure the overall effectiveness of an IR system, one can use *average precision at 11 points of recall*: We determine the precision measures at 11 recall levels 0, 0.1, ..., 1.0 and we calculate their average. For the recall level of 0, the precision is obtained through an interpolation procedure (Baeza-Yates and Ribeiro-Neto, 1999). Another widely accepted measurement is *Mean Average Precision* (*MAP*), defined as follows:

$$\text{MAP} = \frac{1}{M} \sum_{j=1}^{M} \frac{1}{N_j} \sum_{i=1}^{N_j} pr(d_{ij})$$

$$pr(d_{ij}) = \begin{cases} \dfrac{r_{n_i}}{n_i} & \text{if } n_i \leq \text{MAX} \\ 0 & \text{otherwise} \end{cases}$$

Here, n_i denotes the rank of the document d_{ij} in the retrieval result that is relevant to query j; r_{n_i} is the number of relevant documents found up to rank n_i; N_j is the total number of relevant documents for query j; M is the total number of queries and MAX is the cutoff rank (usually set at 1,000 in TREC experiments).

MAP is the most used metric in IR research. However, several other metrics have been proposed. Especially, Discounted Cumulated Gain (DCG) or Normalized Discounted Cumulated Gain (NDCG) (Järvelin and Kekalainen, 2002) are gaining popularity. NDCG is defined as follows:

$$\text{NDCG}(n) = Z_n \sum_{i=1}^{n} \frac{2^{r(i)} - 1}{\log(1+i)}$$

where n is the cut-off, $r(i)$ is the relevance score of the i-th document in the result list and Z_n is a normalization factor so that $NDCG(n) = 1$ for the ideal list of documents. Notice that $r(i)$ does not have to be binary. One can assign a real value relevance score to a document. For example, a document can be assigned a value of 0, 1, 2, 3, or 4 according to whether the document is "irrelevant," "fair," "good," "excellent," or "perfect." If a document is judged by several human evaluators, the average relevance score can be used. In the current search engine industry, NDCG is a measure often preferred to MAP. One can set a relatively small n. For eample, $n = 1$, 5, or 10 are the values often used, because typical users on Web search are interested in the top results.

For CLIR, in addition to the above metrics, one also use the percentage compared to the effectiveness of the monolingual IR. The latter is performed with manually translated queries. As we will see, the retrieval effectiveness of CLIR is usually lower than that of monolingual IR, but there are some exceptions.

The evaluation of an IR system or method is performed using a test collection, which contains a set of documents, a set of queries as well as human relevance judgments, which are considered as the gold standard. The results retrieved by an IR system are compared to the gold standard. We will list some of the test collections for CLIR developed in TREC in Section 1.7.

1.3   LANGUAGE PROBLEMS IN IR

Investigations in IR have been done almost exclusively on European languages for a long time. This situation has dramatically changed, especially with the advent of the World-Wide Web, and we have now sizable document collections in a number of languages. While the basic process of IR developed for European languages can be reused for other languages, different languages also require specific language-dependent processing. In this section, we describe the typical processing on some of the languages on which there are extensive CLIR initiatives.

1.3.1   European Languages
1.3.1.1 Word Stemming

In general IR, documents and queries are submitted to some preprocessing on words in order to discard meaningless morphological variations. Several "standard" stemming algorithms have been developed and widely used, for example, Porter stemmer (Porter, 1980) and Krovetz stemmer (Krovetz, 1993). The Porter algorithm has been extended to several European languages and tools are available for 15 languages on Snowball.[1] Savoy (Savoy, 1993; 1999; 2006; 2007) and his team (Dolamic and Savoy, 2007) have worked extensively on stemming in different European languages, including East European languages such as Hungarian. In general, a stemming process applies some morphological transformation rules to words in order to remove the inflectional variations such as *-ation* in *inform_ation_*.

Instead of creating stemming rules manually, attempts have also been made to learn the rules automatically from the corpus. Moreau et al. (2007) used analogy to learn morphological transformation rules as follows: If one observes that a word *A* (e.g., *connector*) has a variant form *A'* (e.g., *connect*) sharing the same root but with a different inflection, then a word *B* (e.g., *editor*) with the same inflection as *A* could also be transformed into *B'* in a similar way (e.g., *edit*). Šnajder et al. (2008) describes another method to automatically acquire inflection rules and to perform morphological normalization for Croatian.

Due to the "standardization" of terms, stemming sometimes contributes in increasing the retrieval effectiveness. This is, however, not always the case. Current search engines usually do not use aggressive stemming, while in the area of research, stemming is still generally used as a standard preprocessing.

1.3.1.2 Decompounding

In agglutinative languages such as German, Dutch, and Finish, complex words can be compounded from simpler words. For example, the word *hungerstreiks* in German is compounded from two words

---

[1]http://snowball.tartarus.org/.

hunger (hunger) and *streaks* (strikes), while it can also be written as two separate words. Similarly, Literaturnobelpreistrager (Literature Nobel Laureate) can also be written as *Literatur-Nobelpreistrager* and *Literaturnobelpreis-Tragerin*, and *Literaturnobelpreis* (Literature Nobel prize) as *Nobelpreis fur Literatur*. The Dutch word "gekkekoeienziekte" (mad cow disease) is used in one of the test queries in CLEF, but does not appear as a single word in the document collection.

The above multiple expressions of the same concept may lead to possible mismatches between a document and a query if one of them uses the compounded word and the other uses two or more separate words. The decompounding process tries to recognize the constituent words within the compounded words and to represent it by the constituent words. However, ambiguities may occur. For example, the word *hungerstreaks* contains the following possible words in German: *erst, hung, hunger, hungers, hungerst, reik, reiks, streik, streaks*. So, the question is to recognize the correct words that compound it. A simple approach is to use a German dictionary, and identify all the possible words in the compound if the compound is not found in the dictionary. This approach was used in Sheridan and Ballerini (1996). A more sophisticated approach relies on the probability of each word in German $P(w_i)$. Given a compounded word, the goal is to select the most probable constituent words $w_1, \ldots, w_n$ in it, such that:

$$w_1, \ldots, w_n = \arg\max_{w_1 \ldots w_n} \prod_{i=1}^{n} P(w_i)$$

This approach has been used successfully in Chen and Gey (2001, 2002). Instead of the probability of individual words, one can also use other measures such as mutual information to consider certain dependency between the constituent words.

The experiments by Chen and Gey (2002) showed that decompounding is important for German and Dutch: it led to significant improvements in MAP ranging from 4% to more than 13% in both monolingual IR and CLIR. Similar improvements have been observed in Braschler and Ripplinger (2004). Hedlund et al. (2001) examined the effects of compound splitting and the use of *n*-grams for Finish IR. They also found decompounding a necessary step for this language.

McNamee and Mayfield (2004a) have used character *n*-grams for IR in several European languages. The utilization of character *n*-grams to decompose words corresponds to a pseudo-decompounding. This approach does not require any linguistic resource. However, the resulting *n*-grams can be noisy, i.e., some constituent *n*-grams of a word (e.g., the trigrams *sum, ump, mpt, pti, tio* and *ion* from "consumption") can match wrongly those of another word (e.g., "assumption"). In general, the retrieval effectiveness using character *n*-grams for IR in European languages is lower than using word stemming and decompounding.

Attempts have also been made to exploit additional features to help decompounding. For example, Alfonseca et al. (2008) tried to consider several features obtained from Web anchor texts, in addition to the measures used previously, such as frequency, compound probability, and mutual information, to determine the correct decompounding. The experiments on German, Dutch, Danish, Norwegian, Swedish, and Finish showed that for all these languages, the additional Web-related features are useful.

All these studies clearly showed the importance of word decompounding in agglutinative languages. The situation that we will describe in the next section for some Asian languages is even more extreme: no boundary is marked between words. So, a process similar to word decompounding is mandatory.

1.3.2 East Asian Languages

In this section, we only discuss about three following languages: Chinese, Japanese, and Korean (also referred to as CJK languages). These languages share some common heritage due to the historical cultural and linguistic ties between these countries. This fact strongly influenced the characteristics of these languages, namely, the utilization of ideograms (or their transcription in modern Korean and Japanese). We will start this section by describing the Chinese language with respect to the requirement of IR and CLIR. Then some characteristics of Japanese and Korean will be described. Readers may refer to Wong et al. (2009) for a more detailed description on Chinese processing.

1.3.2.1 Chinese and Word Segmentation

Chinese texts are written in ideograms (also called Chinese characters or ideographs). One of the distinct characteristics of Chinese (compared to the Indo-European languages) for IR purposes is the absence of space to delimit words. For example, the following string is the title of a newspaper article:

汶川地震灾区首批自建永久性农房建成入住

(The first self-constructed permanent houses for farmers in the Wenchuan earthquake-stricken area have been completed and put in use.)

One would desire to recognize the following words in this sentence: 汶川 (Wenchuan), 地震 (earthquake), 灾区 (disaster area), 首批 (first batch), 自建 (self-constructed), 永久性 (permanent), 农房 (house of farmer), 建成 (constructed), 入住 (inhabited). However, this task is not trivial due to several reasons:

1. Word boundaries can be set at different positions, yet producing legitimate words, and many combinations of Chinese characters can be words.

   For example, while 汶川 (Wenchuan) and 地震(earthquake) form two correct words in the above sentence, it is also possible that the combination of parts of them 川地 (valley) be used as a word in other situations. In the same way, the two characters from the words 农房 and 建成 could also form a word 房建 (house construction) in other situations. Therefore we need to determine, among all the possible character combinations, the correct ones for a given sentence.

2. Unknown words can often appear in sentences.

Until the reports on the earthquakes in 2008, many would not know that 汶川 is the name of a place. Even if one could guess it from the context in which it is used, one could not expect it to be included in a bilingual dictionary and know how to translate it into other languages. Many proper names would fall in the same situation. In addition, new terms can be more easily created in Chinese due to the fact that each Chinese character bears some meanings and a new combination of them can often be meaningful, too.

3. For IR, the flexibility of word formation in Chinese represents a serious problem in IR.

For example, all the following words are related to house, housing, or building: 农房, 房建, 厂房, 工房, 平房, 楼房, etc. An important problem is to be able to recognize the relationships between them so that documents using a related word can be retrieved.

For Chinese IR, the first intuitive approach is to try to determine the correct words from each sentence. This process is called *word segmentation*. The example given above could be segmented into the following words:

汶川　地震　灾区　首批　自建　永久性　农房　建成　入住

Once this is done on both documents and queries, Chinese IR could use the same approaches as for European languages.

Word segmentation has been studied extensively in the Chinese NLP community for several decades, starting from 1980s. Typical approaches include:

- Dictionary-based approaches: one uses a dictionary containing all the possible words, combined with the longest-matching strategy. That is, when a sequence of characters can be segmented in several ways, the one with the longest words are preferred. For a complete sentence, this also means that we try to identify as few words as possible. This strategy usually works well, although it can also result in wrong words. However, the unknown word problem cannot be considered correctly. Usually, an unknown word is segmented into single characters.
- Dictionary with usage statistics: if word usage statistics is available, then a probability can be assigned to each word. Then the segmentation process can select the sequence of words which has the highest likelihood.
- Using segmented corpora: instead of using a dictionary, one can use a manually segmented corpus. The problem of word segmentation can then be cast as a classification problem,

which tries to determine the correct category of each character (e.g., B—beginning of a word, I—inside a word, or E—end of a word). Different learning approaches and models can be used, such as HMM (Hidden Markov model) (Zhang et al., 2003), conditional random field (Peng et al., 2004), and so on.

In general, with a good dictionary or a reasonably large segmented training corpus, the segmentation accuracy can be high—usually over 90% (Sproat and Emerson, 2003).

The experiments on Chinese IR showed that it is reasonable to use the same approaches as for European languages, directly on word-segmented Chinese queries and documents. However, this does not solve the problems of unknown words and word variations. For example, if the word 汶川 is unknown and is segmented into separate characters, much noise (irrelevant documents) will be retrieved because these characters could be used in documents that do not concern 汶川. On the other hand, when the longest words are used, we are also faced with the problem that it does not match shorter constituent words. For example, if 程序设计 (programming) is segmented as a single word, it will not match the constituent words 程序 (program) and 设计 (design).

To deal with these problems, and also to overcome the unavailability of high-quality Chinese word segmentation tools at the beginning of Chinese IR investigations, *n*-grams of characters are used instead of words. As most Chinese words are formed with two characters, the most appropriate length of *n*-grams is 2. For the earlier example, we would obtain the following overlapping bigrams:

汶川　川地　地震　震灾　灾区　区首　首批　批自　自建　建永　永久　久性　性农
农房　房建　建成　成入　入住

This process is simple and requires no linguistic resource. However, notice that the bigrams could correspond to some incorrect words, such as 川地 (valley) and 房建 (house construction). Nevertheless, these seemingly incorrect words are not always harmful to IR. Indeed, the second incorrect bigrams 房建 (house construction) is strongly related to the meaning of the sentence and its inclusion in the index for this sentence is beneficial. In the same way, unknown words (e.g., 汶川) can also be grouped into a bigram, which is better than segmenting them into single characters.

Extensive experiments have been made to test different segmentation approaches in IR: using words, single characters (unigrams), bigrams, or combinations of them (Kwok and Grunfeld, 1996; Nie and Ren, 1999; Shi et al., 2007; Chen et al., 1997). Although the results vary according to the test collections and retrieval models used, the general observation is that using either words, characters or bigrams, one can obtain quite comparable effectiveness. When several types of index are combined, usually one can obtain better effectiveness. For example, in Nie and Ren (1999), the bigram-based method achieved 0.4162 in MAP on TREC 5/6 Chinese test collection, the word-based approach achieved 0.4300, while the combination of them led to 0.4796.

1.3.2.2 Japanese and Korean

The problems in Japanese are very similar to Chinese. Japanese can be written in three sets of characters: Kanji (i.e., Chinese characters), Katakana, and Hiragana. For example, the sentence "I like sports" is written as "私はスポーツが好きです", where 私(I) and 好(like) are in Kanji, スポーツ(sports) in Katakana and the others in Hiragana. As in Chinese, no space is inserted between words. One is faced with the same problem of segmentation as in Chinese. Similar approaches can be used.

In Korean sentences, spaces are added to separate words in Hangul. For example:

내가 운동을 좋아합니다. (I like sports)

The presence of spaces in Korean may lead one to believe that no word segmentation is required. This is not completely true. Although spaces are usually inserted between words, the insertion of spaces is flexible. For example, the term "computer game" can be written as two words 컴퓨터 게임 or as a single word 컴퓨터게임. Therefore, some segmentation or decompounding is still necessary (Tomlinson, 2004).

The three languages have much in common for IR and CLIR. Similar approaches used for Chinese IR have also been used for Japanese and Korean: using word segmentation or using character *n*-grams (Lee et al., 1999; Ogawa and Matsuda, 1999).

1.3.3 Other Languages

In Arabic language, letters can change the form according to its position within a word. A root word can be extended by prefixes and postfixes to form other words (of different categories). Vowels are often omitted in writing. These specific characteristics require stemming and normalization of letters. Many studies have carried out on IR and CLIR in Arabic language, for example, Darwish and Oard (2002), Kadri and Nie (2006), Larkey et al. (2002), Xu et al. (2002), and Chen and Gey (2002). Most of the studies addressed the problem of word stemming and transliteration between English and Arabic.

More recently, investigations started on IR in Indian languages (Jagarlamudi and Kumaran, 2007), and the first TREC-style experimental workshop was organized in 2008—FIRE.[2] Until now, the studies also focused on word processing (stemming).

There are many more languages that we do not discuss in this book. As the Web has become a forum where many languages are used, the search problems will arise when the documents in a language reaches a critical number. It is foreseeable that investigations in IR in these languages and CLIR with these languages will intensify in the future.

---

[2]http://www.isical.ac.in/~clia/.

1.4 THE PROBLEMS OF CROSS-LANGUAGE INFORMATION RETRIEVAL

As we have mentioned earlier, one of the key problems in IR is related to the multiple representations of a meaning. A document and a query are represented by terms that occur in them, which could be different even though they describe the same meaning. This makes it difficult to match the relevant documents against a query.

The representation problem is even more evident in *cross-language information retrieval* (CLIR) or *multi-lingual information retrieval* (MLIR), where queries and documents are described in different languages. How can we create the same or similar internal representation for them when they concern the same piece of information, but written in different languages? For example, how can we recognize that the following descriptions describe the same piece of information?

> There is a major earthquake in Wenchuan, China in 2008 (*in English*).
> Un tremblement de terre violent à Wenchuan secoue la Chine en 2008 (*in French*).
> 中国汶川08年发生强烈地震。(*in Chinese*).

How can we succeed to find the above information when we request for "major earthquakes in recent years" in 2010?

These examples illustrate the main problems in CLIR and MLIR, that of representing and matching the same piece of information or information need in a comparable manner or within the same representation space, even if they are described in different languages. As we saw earlier, in monolingual IR, one hopes to create a standard representation space by performing word stemming, compounding, or decompounding. For example, the words "computers," "computer," "computing" in English can be transformed to "comput" after stemming. But the same concept is expressed as "计算机" or "电脑" in Chinese, "コンピュータ" in Japanese and "كمبيوتر" in Arabic. These terms are not directly comparable even if they are put into the same representation space. The key problem in CLIR is to develop tools to match such terms in different languages that describe the same or a similar meaning. This can be shown in Figure 1.2, in which two representation spaces for two languages are created, and there is a mapping process between them. This mapping is usually a translation process. We will talk about the translation process in more detail later.

Given the additional mapping or translation process, the general architecture of IR shown in Figure 1.1 should be extended into the following diagram, in which a translation module is added (see Figure 1.3):

The translation module can be used in several ways:

- Mapping the document representation into the query representation space: this approach is often called document translation approach (Oard and Hackett, 1997).

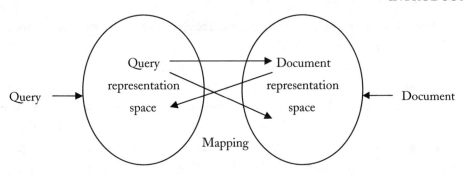

FIGURE 1.2: Mapping between representation spaces,

- Mapping the query representation into the document representation space: this approach is called query translation approach.
- Mapping both document and query representations to a third space (i.e., a pivot language or interlingua) (Ruiz et al., 2000; Kishida and Kando, 2005).

1.4.1 Query Translation vs. Document Translation

It is generally believed that query translation is the most appropriate approach: given a query, the user is allowed to choose the languages of interest, and the query can be translated into the desired languages. In case where the user is capable of understanding the translation(s) of the query, he/she

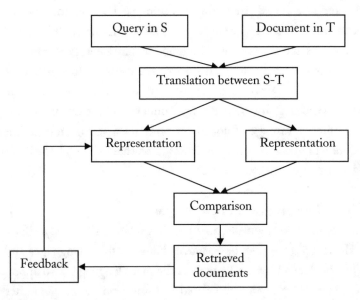

FIGURE 1.3: Typical architecture of a CLIR system.

will be able to correct the translation before it is used to retrieve documents. This approach is flexible and allows for more interactions with the user.

However, query translation often suffers from the problem of translation ambiguity, and this problem is amplified due to the limited amount of context in short queries. From this perspective, document translation seems to be more capable of producing more precise translation due to richer contexts. The availability of efficient MT systems also makes the document translation approach possible. However, it is not obvious that the current MT systems can take full advantage of the existence of richer contexts in document translation. Several studies have compared the query translation and document translation approaches using the same translation tool. For example, Franz et al. (1999) compared the two approaches using the IBM machine translation system. However, no clear advantage has been shown with one approach or another. In the experiments reported in McCarley (1999), McCarley found that the effectiveness is more dependent on the translation direction between languages than query or document translation: French-to-English translation outperforms English-to-French translation, whether it is used in query translation or document translation. All these experiments show that document translation is not necessarily advantageous to query translation. The main reason behind this observation is that the current MT systems exploit only a limited amount of immediate contextual information, and sentences are usually translated independently. The rich contextual information in documents is largely under exploited and does not significantly impact the quality of the translation.

A critical aspect of the document translation approach is that one has to determine in advance to which language each document should be translated and that all the translated versions of the document should be stored. In a truly multilingual IR environment, one would desire to translate each document to all the other languages. This is impracticable because of the multiplication of document versions and the increase in storage requirement. Nevertheless, once a document is pre-translated into the same language as the query, the user can directly read and understand the translated version. Otherwise, a post-retrieval translation is often needed to make the retrieved documents readable by the user (if he/she does not understand the document language).

Due to the limited advantage of document translation shown in experiments, most current research and development on CLIR use query translation due to its high flexibility. In this book, we will also put more focus on query translation.

1.4.2   Using Pivot Language and Interlingua

Direct translation between two languages may not always be possible due to the limitation of translation resources. However, there may be resources between these languages and a third language (e.g., English). This third language can be used as the pivot language. Two approaches are possible: both the document and the query are translated into the pivot language; either the query or the document is translated first to the pivot language, then to the target language. If we extend the first approach, we can also talk about an interlingua approach, i.e., all the documents and queries are translated into this pivot language.

Some researchers have tried to use a pivot language for transitive CLIR. It is shown that this approach can be useful when there is no resource for a direct translation. However, if direct translation resources are available, direct translation usually outperforms transitive translation. We will describe some such experiments in Section 4.4.

As the approaches used to document translation, query translation, and transitive translation are similar, the following description of this book will concentrate on query translation approaches.

1.5   APPROACHES TO TRANSLATION IN CLIR

In addition to the monolingual IR problems, translation is undoubtedly the main problem for CLIR and MLIR. Translation may be required in the following two steps:

1. First, given a query in language A (source language), if the user intends to retrieve documents in language B (target language), terms in language A should be translated to language B, or the reverse, for the retrieval could be performed.
2. Second, once a set of documents in language B are retrieved, the user may also require translating them back to language A, in order to read them.

Despite their great similarity, the above two translation tasks contain much difference. The second translation is a traditional full text translation task, for which automatic Machine Translation (MT) tools are the most appropriate. However, MT is not necessarily the most suitable tool for the first step. There are reasons for this.

- Less strict syntax is required

    The task of translating a query (or document) from a language to another in CLIR is not to make it readable by a human being; rather, its goal is to enable the system (computer) to match the query to documents (or the reverse). Therefore, the translation only has to be usable by the IR system, which is often based on keywords. This means that we do not have to obey the strict language grammar in the target language when producing such a translation, but the selection of translation words is the most important.

- Higher ambiguity

    In the case of query translation, as queries are usually short (typically 2–3 words in Web search), much ambiguity appears. The selection of appropriate translation terms is particularly challenging. This selection problem should be considered not only from the pure translation point of view, but also from the IR point of view, i.e., to match relevant documents in the collection.

- Desired query expansion effect

    The goal of query (document) translation in IR is indeed to produce another representation of the query (document) in a different language. We do not have a unique representation for a meaning, and there may be several possible representations, more or less appropriate for the given context. In order to enable a query to match the documents with different, but equivalent or similar, expressions, it is desirable to include in the translated query all the possible alternative expressions of the meaning. This is indeed a step of *query expansion* often used in monolingual IR, as we explained in Section 1.2.2. This step is often implicitly or explicitly involved in query translation approaches. The requirement of query expansion makes the translation process in CLIR different from the traditional full text translation process, which aims at producing a unique translation for a given sentence.

- Term weighting

    Term weighting is important in IR. Weights assigned to each of the terms in a query aim to reflect the importance of the term for the matching process. For CLIR, it is also desirable to associate weights to translation terms. Such a weight reflects not only the importance of the term in the query, but also the appropriateness of the translation. This term weighting aspect is specific to IR and is not involved in MT.

The above differences show that translation in CLIR is not a traditional translation task, but a translation task intimately embedded in IR. Although translation in CLIR shares many of the problems in general translation, it also has its own problems, and can be dealt with in a different way. In CLIR literature, in addition to full text machine translation, the following two approaches are also widely proposed and tested:

- Dictionary-based translation: this approach tries to identify and select the possible translations of each source word from a bilingual dictionary. The translation words form together a representation of the query in the target language.

- Translation based on parallel corpora: a parallel corpus contains both source language texts and their translations in the target language. Approaches that exploit a parallel corpus try to extract the strong translation relations between the two languages, ether at the word level or at a higher level (e.g., phrase level). These translation relations can then be used to translate queries or documents.

Notice that the above classification does not create a strict boundary between different approaches to translation. For example, statistical MT approaches also exploit parallel corpora. So, there is much in common between statistical MT and the third class of approaches. However, by separating the approaches using MT systems, we want to stress the fact that MT systems are often used as a black box. The three families of approaches will be described in more detail.

1.6 THE NEED FOR CROSS-LANGUAGE AND MULTILINGUAL IR

Although the utility of monolingual IR no longer needs to be justified—one only has to think about the widely spread uses of search engines, it may not appear obvious to some people that users may need to find information in languages other than their native language.

As we stated earlier, the primary goal of an information seeker is to identify relevant information itself. The form of the description of the information is usually of less importance (provided that the user can understand it). For example, a piece of information can be described in a text, a table, a picture, and also in different languages. So, in principle, any piece of relevant information, in whatever language, could be judged relevant to the user. However, pieces of information become useful only when they are understandable by the user. The obstacle to understand documents in a different language is the very reason why most current search engines only provide monolingual retrieval functionality and why most users are only interested in documents in their native languages. However, this obstacle is being lowered due to the progress made in automatic translation tools: for a number of languages, translation tools allow users to understand or to gist the contents of a document in a different language.

Independently from the available translation tools, there are also needs for users to retrieve documents regardless to languages. Below are some examples of such situations.

- The relevant information can be in a form (e.g., image) that is directly understandable by the user, even if it is also described in a different language. This is the case of multimedia information retrieval, in which the multimedia information can also be described or annotated in a different language. When the user intends to find a relevant image on some subject (e.g., picture of moon eclipse), it is not important whether the image is described or annotated in the user's native language. What is important is the image itself. Multimedia IR may or may not be related to MLIR and CLIR, depending on the technique used to identify the appropriate images. The case that is related to MLIR and CLIR is when we use the textual description of image to determine if the image is relevant, and the textual description is in a language different from that of the query (also a textual description). Notice that the current image (and other media) retrieval methods are largely based on the textual description. So there is indeed a need to employ techniques of CLIR to identify relevant images that are described in a different language.

- The desired relevant information may not exist in the user's native language. For example, an English speaking traveler who desires to find information about "the Folkloric Art Festival in Handan" (a medium size city in China) may not find any relevant information in English, and relevant information may be provided in Chinese only. To find this information the user's query has to be translated into Chinese (or the documents be translated into English). We are concerned here with the problem of CLIR.

- The description in documents can mix up several languages. For example, a document in Chinese can describe "因特网的进化" (evolution of Internet) only in Chinese or using both English and Chinese words as in "Internet的进化". In the same way, a Japanese document can also describe this concept as "Internetの進化" or "インターーネットの進化". It is desirable that some form of multilingual IR capability is provided to retrieve these documents.

- The user may intend to find all the relevant information available, whatever the language is used. This is a case of recall-oriented retrieval. A typical case is patent retrieval: When a patent professional tries to identify if there is an existing patent for a technology or invention, he/she should not limit the search in only one language, and should extend it to many other languages. Another typical situation is when a company tries to identify if there is an international competitor or collaborator in the same business sector, the search should not be limited within the same country and the same language.

- Finally, there are a quite large percentage of users who understand more than one language. Part of these users can read documents in a different language without feeling comfortable to formulate correct queries in it. A CLIR tool is of much help to them. Another part of the users can be fluent in several languages. A CLIR and MLIR tool could still be useful by removing from them the burden of formulating the query several times in several languages.

The above situations tend to occur more frequently due to the ever frequent communications between different language communities. The technical developments in these areas also provide readily usable technologies to implement such systems effectively. We are at the edge of viewing such systems available for public uses. Yet problems still remain, and there are rooms for further improvements. The goal of this book is to provide a description of the techniques proposed for CLIR and MLIR, as well as the remaining problems that need to be solved.

1.7   THE HISTORY OF CLIR

Although the majority of studies in IR concern monolingual IR, CLIR problems attracted research interests from as early as 1960s (for example, Salton, 1970). Since then, a number of attempts have been made on CLIR and MLIR, in particular, in the area of library science. Readers can find a summary of the early attempts in this area in (Oard and Dorr, 1996).

Research in CLIR seriously took off from mid-1990s when World-Wide Web started to be popular. Documents in English and other languages became publicly available. Even though the majority of searches on the Web was (and still is) monolingual, there were needs for retrieving documents in other languages. Investigations became intensified from 1997 when CLIR experiments were officially conducted in TREC-6 (Text REtrieval Conference)[3] organized by the National Institute of Standards and Technology (NIST) (Voorhees and Harman, 1997). Even earlier in TREC-4 and TREC-5, while retrieval experiments on Spanish documents were conducted, some groups (Davis and Dunning, 1995) already carried out experiments on several ways to translate queries from English to Spanish. More CLIR experiments have been carried out between more European languages since TREC-7: English, French, German, Italian, Dutch, and so on. Table 1.2 summarizes the monolingual IR on languages other than English and CLIR experiments in TREC.

CLIR experiments on European languages started in CLEF (Cross-Language Experiment Forum)[4] in 2000. The first experiments dealt with English, German, French, and Italian documents using queries in Dutch, English, French, German, Italian, Spanish, Swedish, and Finnish. Then more and more languages were added in the following years: Spanish, Dutch, Swedish, Finish, Portuguese, Russian, Bulgarian, Hungarian, and so on. From 2005, multilingual retrieval has been conducted on a Web collection—EuroGov—collected from a number of government websites in Europe. In CLEF 2007, Indian languages are studied: Hindi, Telugu, and Marathi.

The NTCIR[5] series of workshops started in 1999. They are organized by the National Institute for Informatics (NII) of Japan. They focus on Asian languages, in addition to English: Japanese, Chinese, and Korean. New Asian languages are also being considered: Vietnamese, Mongolian, and so on.

In addition to the above experiments on CLIR, there are also initiatives to develop methods for IR in different languages. For example, a series of experiments on Chinese Web IR have been organized by Peking University[6] since 2004. Forum for Information Retrieval Evaluation (FIRE)[7] started in 2008, aiming at testing IR and CLIR techniques for Indian languages: Hindi, Bangla, Marathi, Tamil, Telugu, Punjabi, and Malayalam.

All these experiments have triggered a tremendous amount of research work on CLIR and MLIR and contributed significantly to the development of new techniques for CLIR and MLIR. If CLIR effectiveness (measured in terms of mean average precision—MAP) was much lower than that of monolingual IR at the beginning (around 50%), the difference between them has been much

---

[3] http://trec.nist.gov.

[4] http://www.clef-campaign.org/.

[5] http://research.nii.ac.jp/ntcir/.

[6] http://net.pku.edu.cn/~webg/cwt/.

[7] http://www.isical.ac.in/~clia/.

TREC	LANGUAGES AND DOCUMENT COLLECTIONS	QUERIES
	TABLE 1.2: CLIR experiments in TREC.	
TREC-3 (1994)	Spanish (monolingual): *El Norte* Newspaper	SP 1-25 (Spanish)
TREC-4 (1995)	Spanish (monolingual): *El Norte* Newspaper	SP 26-50 (Spanish)
TREC-5 (1996)	Spanish (monolingual): *El Norte* newspaper and *Agence France Presse* Chinese (monolingual): *Xinhua News agency, People's Daily*	SP 51-75 (Spanish) CH 1-28 (Chinese)
TREC-6 (1997)	Chinese (monolingual): The same documents as TREC-6 CLIR: English: *Associated Press* French, German: *Schweizerische Depeschenagentur (SDA)*	CH 29-54 (Chinese) CL 1-25 (English, French)
TREC-7 (1998)	CLIR: English, French, German, Italian: *Schweizerische Depeschenagentur (SDA)* + German: *New Zurich Newspaper (NZZ)*	CL 26-53 (Several languages)
TREC-8 (1999)	CLIR in English, French, German, Italian: The same document sets as in TREC-7	CL 54-81 (Several languages)
TREC-9 (2000)	English-Chinese: Chinese newswire articles from Hong Kong	CH 55-79 (English, Chinese)
TREC 2001	English-Arabic: Arabic newswire from *Agence France Presse*	1-25 (English, Arabic)
TREC 2002	English-Arabic: Arabic newswire from *Agence France Presse*	26-75 (English, Arabic)

reduced. In the current state of the art for well-studied languages, CLIR's effectiveness is close to that of monolingual IR. This shows the maturity of CLIR techniques. Another sign of the maturity of technologies of CLIR and MLIR is the fact that commercial companies started to offer products for them. For example, Yahoo! started to offer multilingual search from 2006. It allows automatically translating queries in French and German to four other languages—English, Spanish, Italian and French/German to retrieve documents in these languages. Google also started to offer CLIR facilities for a number of languages from 2007. First, the user's query is translated to one of the target languages. The retrieved documents in the latter language are then translated back to the query language using an MT system. The quality of the translations by Yahoo! and Google is variable according to the topic areas and the language. However, these tools allow the users to access more easily the documents written in different languages and to get a quick idea of their contents. They provide the prerequisite for practical uses of CLIR.

In the following chapters, we will describe the techniques proposed in the literature to deal with the CLIR problems.

·　·　·　·

CHAPTER 2

Using Manually Constructed Translation Systems and Resources for CLIR

For a long time, people have been manually constructing various translation systems and resources. These include machine translation (MT) systems (e.g., Systran) and machine-readable bilingual dictionaries (MRD) and thesauri.

MT systems are constructed for the primary purpose of providing full-text translation without any manual intervention. The quality of translation has been much improved, now compared to the early age of MT. Although MT results are not perfect, they are often understandable by human readers. One may believe that if full text MT systems are available, they are the ideal tools for document or query translation in CLIR: one can simply submit a document or a query to an MT system to obtain its translation. Then the remaining problem is just the same as in monolingual IR.

Is it really that simple? In this chapter, we will describe some representative experiments using MT systems, and the problems that this approach raises. It will turn out that off-the-shelve MT system such as Systran provide little flexibility to accommodate the specific need of CLIR. People then turned to bilingual dictionaries, whose open nature allows one to integrate various term weighting and selection methods for the specific purposes of CLIR. We will see that this approach can be as effective as the method using a high-quality MT system (e.g., Systran, Logos). In the second part of this chapter, we will describe the approaches based on bilingual dictionaries.

2.1 MACHINE TRANSLATION

Let us start with a brief description of the state of the art of machine translation (MT). Although there are often hybrid systems, we can generally classify MT systems into two categories: traditional rule-based MT and statistical MT (SMT). Systran[1] is a typical rule-based MT system. The MT systems of Google[2] and Language Weaver[3] are statistical systems. Rule-based systems operate

[1]http://www.systransoft.com.
[2]http://translate.google.com.
[3]http://www.languageweaver.com.

using rules and resources constructed manually. Rules and resources can be of different types: lexical, phrasal, syntactic, semantic, and so on. For example, translations stored in a bilingual dictionary provide basic resources for lexical translation. Phrases and their translations can also be stored in a dictionary in addition to single words. For example, the compound term in French "pomme de terre" and its English translation "potato" should be stored in the dictionary to produce a correct translation of it. Grammatical or syntactic rules allow one to recognize the syntactic structure of the source language and to generate the corresponding structure in the target language. For example, a French structure "NN1 de NN2" is often translated into English as "NN2' NN1'," where NN1 and NN2 are common nouns and NN1' and NN2' their translations in English. An English sentence with the structure Subject–Verb–Object should be translated into Japanese as Subject–Object–Verb. Semantic rules aim at helping select the correct translation for the sense used in the source language when ambiguity occurs. For example, to arrive at the correct translation of the word "drug" into other languages, it is important to understand what it means: illegal substance or legal medication. However, semantic rules are also the most difficult to set up and to integrate into the translation process. A complete semantic modeling of a language would require a large amount of semantic information, which would be equivalent to a modeling of world knowledge. This is difficult to achieve in practice. So, only limited semantic information is used in MT for a set of words that are recognized to be highly ambiguous.

SMT are built on statistical language and translation models, which are extracted automatically from large set of texts and their translations (parallel texts). The extracted elements can concern words, word n-grams, phrases, etc. in both languages as well as the translations between them.

2.1.1 Rule-Based MT

Traditional rule-based MT approaches usually follow what is called Vauquois triangle (Vauquois 1968) (see Figure 2.1.):

One can distinguish four levels of approaches in this triangle. At the lowest level, a source-language sentence is translated directly word-by-word to the target language (direct translation approach). Basically, in this approach, one uses a bilingual dictionary to determine the potential translation word(s) or expression(s) for each word. The source words are replaced by the translation candidates, and some modifications can possibly be made on words or word sequences to account for word order and grammatical agreements in the target language. This approach marks the first generation of MT systems in 1950s–1960s. It is not difficult to see that this simple approach cannot deal with the high complexity of natural languages. For example, it cannot account for the fact that the translation of words strongly depends on the context in which they appear, and some words or expressions in a language cannot be translated into the target language by a single word or expression.

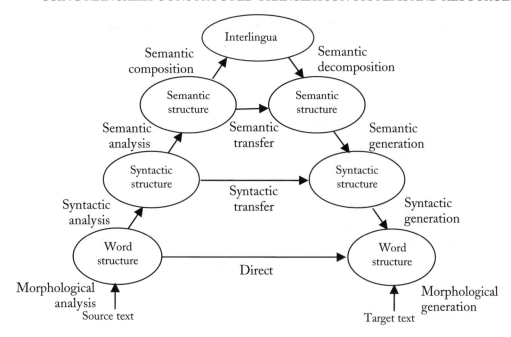

FIGURE 2.1: Vauquois triangle (Vauquois 1968).

The second and third levels of MT use transfer approaches: syntactic or semantic trans-fer. This approach first analyzes the source-language sentence to recognize the syntactic/semantic structure and the words. Then the structure is transferred to a structure in the target language. Finally, the target-language sentence is generated by putting the translation words and expressions into the proper structure in the target-language.

Finally, the fourth level approach is called interlingual approach. This approach tries to create a language-independent representation for a sentence (in interlingua). Then the translation in the target language is just to express the interlingua representation in the target language (the genera-tion process).

Theoretically, the interlingua approach has many advantages over the transfer approaches: one does not have to write specific transfer rules between every pair of languages (there are n^2 such pairs for n languages), but only has to translate between each language and the interlingua (there are thus $2n$ such translations). However, the assumption of this approach is that one is able to rep-resent sentences in every language in a standard interlingual representation. Although there have been attempts to implement the interlingua approach (Dorr et al., 2004), the creation of such an interlingual representation turned out to be a very difficult enterprise in practice.

Most current state-of-the-art rule-based MT systems use transfer approaches. We can see this in the representative Systran system. Hutchins and Somers (1992) and Hutchins (1986) summarize the following main processing steps of Systran:

1. format identification of the source text,
2. identification of idiomatic forms,
3. lookup into the principal dictionary,
4. morphological analysis and detection of unknown words,
5. identification of compounds/phrases with the help of a limited semantic dictionary,
6. resolution of homograph (e.g., "states" as noun or verb),
7. segmentation of sentence into clauses,
8. identification of simple syntactic relations (noun-adjective tense, etc.),
9. disambiguation of number (e.g., to recognize that "control" is on "smog and pollution" in "smog and pollution control is . . ."),
10. determine subject–predicate,
11. deep syntactic analysis,
12. conditional transfer of idioms,
13. translation of prepositions,
14. structural transfer,
15. default translation of the other words,
16. morphological generation,
17. Final arrangement (e.g., transforming "le homme" to "l'homme" in French).

As we can see, most of the operations are at lexical and syntactic levels, and very limited semantic information is used. This gives rise to the translation ambiguity problem: if the ambiguity cannot be solved by syntactic information and is not covered by phrase or idiom dictionaries, then there is a high chance that the word will be translated by its default translation. This may lead to wrong translations. We will see several examples later in the next section where we discuss about the potential problems of using MT systems for CLIR.

2.1.2   Statistical MT

Statistical MT relies on translation examples contained in a parallel corpus, i.e., a set of texts translated into another language. Such a corpus can be further processed into aligned sentences (see Chapter 3). From such parallel texts, various types of translation relationship can be extracted and used to translate new texts. Most current work on SMT is based on, or extended from, the IBM models (Brown et al., 1993). This family of translation models is based on noisy channel: the problem of translation is considered as that of determining a target-language (English) sentence $\hat{\mathbf{e}}$ that corresponds best to the source-language (French) sentence $\mathbf{f}$. This corresponds to the following formulation:

$$\hat{\mathbf{e}} = \arg\max_{\mathbf{e}} P(\mathbf{e}\,|\,\mathbf{f})$$

$$= \arg\max_{\mathbf{e}} \frac{P(\mathbf{f}\,|\,\mathbf{e}) \times P(\mathbf{e})}{P(\mathbf{f})}$$

$$= \arg\max_{\mathbf{e}} P(\mathbf{f}\,|\,\mathbf{e}) \times P(\mathbf{e})$$

In the above equation, $P(\mathbf{f}|\mathbf{e})$, called *translation model*, encodes the translation probability from $\mathbf{e}$ to $\mathbf{f}$, and $P(\mathbf{e})$, called *language model,* denotes the likelihood of the sentence $\mathbf{e}$ in the target language. Both $\mathbf{e}$ and $\mathbf{f}$ are further decomposed into smaller elements than sentences. $P(\mathbf{e})$ is usually estimated by an *n*-gram model. For $P(\mathbf{f}|\mathbf{e})$, Brown et al. (1993) assumes that we have a set A of possible alignments between the words in the two sentences, and we have:

$$P(\mathbf{f}\,|\,\mathbf{e}) = \sum_{\mathbf{a} \in A(\mathbf{e},\mathbf{f})} P(\mathbf{f},\mathbf{a}\,|\,\mathbf{e})$$

where $\mathbf{a}$ is one possible alignment between words in the two sentences. Denoting such an alignment by

$$\mathbf{a} = (a_1,\ldots,a_m) \text{ with } a_i \in [0,l] \; \forall i \in [1,m], \; l = |\mathbf{e}|, \; m = |\mathbf{f}|$$

where a_i is the position of the word in the sentence $\mathbf{e}$ that aligns with the word of position i in the sentence $\mathbf{f}$. For example, $a_2 = 3$ means that the French word at position 2 in $\mathbf{f}$ is aligned to the English word at position 3 in $\mathbf{e}$. Notice that the $\mathbf{e}$ is augmented by an empty word NULL (assumed to be at position 0) to account for the fact that some words in $\mathbf{f}$ cannot be aligned to any word in $\mathbf{e}$. In this case, these words are aligned to NULL. The following figure shows one possible word alignment between two sentences in English and French:

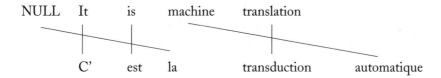

This alignment corresponds to $\mathbf{a}=(1, 2, 0, 4, 3)$.

In general, $P(\mathbf{f}, \mathbf{a}|\mathbf{e})$ can be written into the following form:

$$P(\mathbf{f},\mathbf{a}\,|\,\mathbf{e}) = P(m\,|\,\mathbf{e})\prod_{j=1}^{m} P(a_j\,|\,a_1^{j-1},f_1^{j-1},m,\mathbf{e})P(f_j\,|\,a_1^{j},f_1^{j-1},m,\mathbf{e})$$

The above formula can be read as follows: $P(\mathbf{f}, \mathbf{a}|\mathbf{e})$ is determined by trying to determine:

1. the length m of the sentence $\mathbf{f}$ to which $\mathbf{e}$ can be translated, i.e., $P(m|\mathbf{e})$;
2. the probability to align each position j in the sentence $\mathbf{f}$ to a position a_j in the sentence $\mathbf{e}$, given the previous alignments and translation words, i.e., $P(a_j | a_1^{j-1}, f_1^{j-1}, m, \mathbf{e})$;
3. and the probability to fill in the position j by the word f_j, i.e., $P(f_j | a_1^{j}, f_1^{j-1}, m, \mathbf{e})$.

The above three probabilities can be further defined in different ways by making some simplifications. Here, we will focus on the simplest model—model 1 because this is the most often used model in CLIR.

In IBM model 1, it is assumed that

1. A source sentence can be translated into a sentence of any length equiprobably, i.e., $P(m \mid \mathbf{e})$ is a constant $P(m \mid \mathbf{e}) = \varepsilon$;
2. A position j in the sentence $\mathbf{f}$ can be aligned to any position in the source sentence equiprobably, i.e., $P(a_j | a_1^{j-1} f_1^{j-1}, m, \mathbf{e}) = 1/(l+1)$;
3. The probability to fill in a word at position j in $\mathbf{f}$ is only dependent on the corresponding English word e_{a_j}, i.e., $P(f_j | a_1^{j}, f_1^{j-1}, m, \mathbf{e}) = t(f_j | e_{a_j})$

where $t(f_j | e_{a_j})$ is the word translation probability from e_{a_j} to f_j.

Then we have the following simplified formula:

$$P(\mathbf{f}, \mathbf{a} | \mathbf{e}) = \varepsilon \times \prod_{j=1}^{m} \frac{t(f_j | e_{a_j})}{l+1} = \frac{\varepsilon}{(l+1)^m} \times \prod_{j=1}^{m} t(f_j | e_{a_j})$$

The above formula determines the likelihood that a sentence $\mathbf{f}$ corresponds to $\mathbf{e}$ through the alignment $\mathbf{a}$. Summing up all the alignments $\mathbf{a}$, we have:

$$p(\mathbf{f} | \mathbf{e}) = \frac{\varepsilon}{(l+1)^m} \sum_{a_1=0}^{l} \cdots \sum_{a_m=0}^{l} \prod_{j=1}^{m} t(f_j | e_{a_j})$$

$$= \frac{\varepsilon}{(l+1)^m} \prod_{j=1}^{m} \sum_{i=0}^{l} t(f_j | e_i)$$

This formula uses the word translation probability $t(f_j | e_{a_j})$, which is undefined before we exploit the parallel corpus. In fact, one of the goals of the exploitation is precisely to define such a function. To do this, we use the Expectation Maximization (EM) algorithm (Dempster et al., 1977), whose goal is to determine a function $t(f_j | e_{a_j})$ such that it can maximize the alignment probability between the given aligned sentence pairs in the parallel corpus. The EM process iterates on E-step (expectation) and M-step (maximization), which update the following quantities until convergence (see (Brown et al., 1993) for details of their derivation):

E-step:

$$c(f|e; \mathbf{e}^{(s)}, \mathbf{f}^{(s)}) = \sum_{\mathbf{a}} P(\mathbf{a} | \mathbf{e}^{(s)}, \mathbf{f}^{(s)}) \sum_{j=1}^{m} \delta(f, f_j) \delta(e, e_{a_j})$$

$$= \frac{t(f|e)}{\sum_{i=0}^{l} t(f|e_i)} \sum_{j=1}^{m} \delta(f, f_j) \sum_{i=0}^{l} \delta(e, e_i)$$

M-step:

$$\lambda_e = \sum_{f} \sum_{s=1}^{S} c(f|e; \mathbf{e}^{(s)}, \mathbf{f}^{(s)})$$

$$t(f|e) = \lambda_e^{-1} \sum_{s=1}^{S} c(f|e; \mathbf{e}^{(s)}, \mathbf{f}^{(s)})$$

where $(\mathbf{e}^{(s)}, \mathbf{f}^{(s)})$ $(1 \leq s \leq S)$ is a pair of aligned sentences, δ is the Kronecker delta function (i.e., $\delta(x,y) = 1$ iff $x=y$).

It is possible that the EM process gets trapped at a local maximum. Fortunately for IBM model 1, it turns out that the local maximum is the global maximum, so we do not have this problem. However, for more sophisticated models, we do have such a problem. The solution one uses is to start from a lower level model to train a higher-order model. For example, we can train a model 1, use it as the starting point for the training of a model 2, which is then used to train model 3, and so on.

In more sophistical models, the translation relationships between words in the source sentence and target sentence are not translated independently from their position. Word position is taken into account in IBM model 2. Word order can change during the translation. For example, "solar system" is translated as "système solaire" in French in which the word order is reversed. This is modeled by a factor called distortion. A word in a language can also be translated by more than one word in the target language. This is modeled by fertility. For example, the word "potato" is translated by three words "pomme de terre" in French. So the fertility of "potato" is 3. Distortion and fertility are incorporated in IBM models 3 and 4. We will not describe the details of these models, as they are not often used in CLIR. Interested readers can refer to Knight (1999), Manning and Schütze (1999) and Brown et al. (1993) for details.

In more recent SMT studies, phrases are considered (Kohen et al., 2003). The observation that motivates phrase-based MT is the fact that many phrases cannot be translated word-by-word into another language, and they should be translated as a unit. This is the case for the French term "pomme de terre" (potato), which would be translated into "apple of soil" if it is translated in a word-by-word manner. Typically, for phrases whose translation is not compositional, i.e., cannot be composed from the translation of their components, it is necessary to perform phrase translation.

Phrase-based SMT extends from the previous word-based SMT models by trying to align phrases in the parallel corpus. More specifically, the translation model $P(\mathbf{f}|\mathbf{e})$ is determined by the translation between phrases in $\mathbf{e}$ and in $\mathbf{f}$. To do this, the sentence $\mathbf{f}$ is first segmented into phrases, i.e., $\bar{f}_1, \ldots, \bar{f}_M$ and $\bar{e}_1, \ldots, \bar{e}_M$. A phrase is a consecutive sequence of words (which could be a single word or NULL). Then each phrase $\bar{f}_i$ is translated to an English phrase $\bar{e}_i$. Assuming a translation probability $\phi(\bar{f}_i \mid \bar{e}_i)$, the translation model is then defined as follows:

$$P(\mathbf{f} \mid \mathbf{e}) = \prod_{i=1}^{M} \phi(\bar{f}_i \mid \bar{e}_i) d(a_i - b_{i-1})$$

where $d(a_i - b_{i-1})$ is a distortion function, modeling the reordering in the output phrases $\bar{e}_i$, with a_i being the start position of $\bar{f}_i$ and b_{i-1} the end position of $\bar{f}_{i-1}$.

In order to favor translation into longer sentences, an additional factor $\omega^{length(\mathbf{e})}$ is added in the following equation, where ω is usually set at a larger value than 1:

$$\mathbf{e} = \arg\max_{\mathbf{e} \in E} P(\mathbf{f} \mid \mathbf{e}) \times P(\mathbf{e}) \times \omega^{length(\mathbf{e})}$$

The phrase translation model is also estimated from a parallel corpus, as word-based translation model. However, phrases are not given before hand. They are determined during the training process using some heuristics. In Kohen et al. (2003), several strategies are compared, among them, the following ones:

- in a pair of parallel sentences, the words within a source-language phrase should be aligned to words within the corresponding target-language phrase;
- a phrase should correspond to a certain syntactic structures (a sub tree in the parsing result).

The first heuristic is used on top of a word alignment (using an IBM model). Then the corresponding blocks of words in parallel sentences, which comply with the heuristic, are considered to be aligned phrases. At the end, a phrase translation table is obtained. Some variants of this strategy are also tested: using word alignments in both directions (from source-language to target-language and the reverse) and considering either the intersection or the union of the corresponding blocks in both cases as aligned phrases.

In addition, the second heuristic requires a parsing to recognize the syntactic structure of sentences. Only phrases that correspond to a sub tree in the parsing tree are retained.

In the experiments of Kohen et al. (2003), it is found that using phrase-based SMT, one can obtain significantly higher BLEU score (Papineni et al., 2001) on a set of test phrases than word-based SMT methods. However, the addition of the second heuristic does not help further. On the contrary, it harms the performance. The reason is that by using this heuristic, only a small number of phrases are retained, and many useful sequence of words (phrase according to the first strategy), such as "there is," "note that," do not correspond to a sub tree in the parsing result.

The training of IBM models has been implemented in several toolkits. GIZA++ (Och and Ney, 2003) is now widely used for it.

For the purpose of SMT (i.e., to generate a complete translation of a sentence), we also need a decoder to determine the best sequence of words in the target language. This corresponds to argmax in the earlier equation. Beam search and Viterbi search are two typical approaches used in this process (Manning and Schütze, 1999). For CLIR, the goal is not to generate a correct sentence in the target language, but the selection of appropriate translation terms. Therefore, we will not describe the decoding process here.

2.2   BASIC UTILIZATION OF MT IN CLIR

The basic approach to use an MT system in CLIR is simple: one just has to submit either the query (in query translation strategy) or the documents (in document translation strategy) to an MT system to obtain a translated version. Then the translated version is used as a query in monolingual IR.

For instance, if we submit the query "Destruction of the tropical forest in South America" to Systran, it is translated to "Destruction de la forêt tropicale en Amérique du Sud," which seems a perfect translation. This translation in French can be used to retrieve documents in a French document collection. In the same way, we can also perform document translation. This is feasible given the high efficiency of the current MT systems.

Looking at the above example, one may think that the translation problem in CLIR is correctly solved. However, things can go wrong. A sentence can be translated by wrong translation terms.

To provide concrete examples of query translations by MT systems, we show below the translations by Systran and Logos MT systems for some queries used in TREC-6 CLIR experiments:

Query #3 What measures are being taken to stem international drug traffic?
Query #9 What effects has logging had on desertification?

Systran translation:

> Quelles mesures sont prises au trafic de stupéfiants international de tige?
> Quels effets l'enregistrement a-t-il eus sur la désertification?

Logos translation

> Quelles mesures sont prises pour contenir la circulation de médicament internationale?
> Quels effets l'inscription ont porté le? desertification?

All the above translations have some problems. In the translation by Systran, the term "stem" is incorrectly translated as "tree stem," and the ambiguous word "logging" is wrongly translated in the meaning of "registration." While in Logos translation, the term "drug" is incorrectly translated to "médicament" (legal medication), and the term "logging" is also translated incorrectly. In addition, "desertification" is unknown (and left untranslated).

The above examples are quite typical when using MT systems for query translation: When correct translation terms are selected, the translated queries are readable, and correct meaning is described. In other cases, when a term is wrongly selected, the query can drift from the original meaning, and the retrieval result will contain much noise (irrelevant documents).

The key problem for query translation in CLIR is the incorrect selection of translation words for ambiguous words. This problem is difficult to solve, and the difficulty is amplified by the fact that queries are short and not much contextual information is available to help select the appropriate translation words.

The above examples are translated using rule-based MT systems. One may think that more recent SMT systems, such as Google translation system, could perform better than the traditional rule-based MT systems, because they can exploit better the immediate context in which the ambiguous word appears. Indeed, phrases and immediate context are incorporated in modern SMT systems. This may lead to a more appropriate selection of translation words in some cases. For example, the fact that the word "traffic" appears with "drug" provides an indication (in the translation model) that "drug" should be translated into "drogue" or "stupéfiant" in French. However, the basic problems still remain. The translation model often fails to take advantage of the contextual information due to several reasons. Current statistical translation models are limited in the scope of the context considered: they often take into account only the immediate context. They do not consider distant dependencies. If the meaning of an ambiguous word depends on a distant word, SMT may fail to account for it. In addition, models used in SMT rely on a set of characteristics observed on the training examples. These characteristics may fail to capture the linguistic phenomena (especially the semantic information) that govern the translation in many cases. As a consequence, the trained translation model is not powerful enough to propose appropriate translations in these cases.

Let us use a set of possible queries containing the ambiguous word "drug" to illustrate the possible problems with both rule-based and statistical MT systems. We use Systran and Google as representative translation systems and the queries are translated from English to French and Chinese. The translations are provided in the following table 2.1. The translation words for "drug" are underlined in the examples. We also indicate whether the translation is correct. In some cases, the translation is indicated as "possible" because the original query is ambiguous even for a human being. Thus several translations are possible.

The translation of the ambiguous word "drug" is extremely difficult for MT systems. As we can see, in some cases, the correct translation is chosen, and in some other cases, the incorrect translation is chosen. Let us analyze these examples in more detail.

2.2.1   Rule-Based MT

Rule-based MT relies much on the phrase dictionary, and sometimes on semantic information, to determine the correct translation of an ambiguous word. If the ambiguous word "drug" is part of a phrase, whose translation is stored in the dictionary, then a rule-based MT system will be able to select the correct translation. It is likely the case that "drug traffic" is stored as a phrase in Systran and it is translated as a whole (although it is difficult to be certain about this, as we do not have the insider information about this system).

For other cases, the situation is different. It seems that the other queries such as "drug insurance" and "drug research" (which concern legal medication) are not recognized as phrases by Systran. In these cases, words are first translated separately; then the translations are grouped together. This may lead to the utilization of the most common translation word to translate the ambiguous word, specified as default translation in Step 15 in Systran's process (assuming here that no further information is available to change this choice). According to the examples produced by Systran, it seems that the most common translation of "drug" in French is "drogue" (illegal substance), but "药物" (legal medication) in Chinese. For "drug insurance," "drug research" and all the other examples, the word "drug" is simply translated by the most common translation word identified in the dictionary. In some cases, the default translation is correct, but not in other cases. The translation in French provided by Systran for examples 2, 3, and 4 are incorrect, as the queries are not related to illegal substance, but to legal medication. On the other hand, the default translation of the word in Chinese is correct for these examples.

The examples 5 and 6 are highly ambiguous even for humans. It is difficult to judge which translation is correct. These examples stress once again the ambiguity problems with short queries. In these cases, without user's intervention, it is difficult to guess the intended meaning of the word "drug." Any translation tool will suffer from this fact.

TABLE 2.1: Translation examples with Systran and Google translation systems.

SYSTRAN TRANSLATION	GOOGLE TRANSLATION
1. drug traffic	
trafic de <u>stupéfiants</u> (correct) 毒品交易 (correct)	trafic de <u>stupéfiants</u> (correct) 毒品贩运 (correct)
2. drug insurance:	
assurance de <u>drogue</u> (incorrect) 药物保险 (correct)	d'assurance <u>médicaments</u> (correct) 药物保险 (correct)
3. drug research:	
recherche de <u>drogue</u> (incorrect) 药物研究 (correct)	la recherche sur les <u>drogues</u> (incorrect) 药物研究 (correct)
4. drug for treatment of Friedreich's ataxia:	
<u>drogue</u> pour le traitement de l'ataxie de Friedreich (incorrect for the word "drug") Friedreich的不整齐的治疗的<u>药物</u> (correct only for the words "drug" and "treatment")	<u>médicament</u> pour le traitement de l'Ataxie de Friedreich (correct) 药物治疗弗里德的共济失调 (correct except for Friedreich)
5. drug control:	
commande de <u>drogue</u> (possibly correct for "drug" but incorrect for "control") 药物管制 (possible)	contrôle des <u>drogues</u> (possible) 药物管制 (possible)
6. drug production:	
production de <u>drogue</u> (possible) 药物生产 (possible)	la production de <u>drogues</u> (possible) 药物生产 (possible)

2.2.2   Statistical MT

For Google using SMT, the selection of the translation word depends on, on the one hand, the frequency that a word is translated by a translation, and on the other hand, the immediate context around the word to be translated. The latter context is taken into account by using phrase-based SMT and the language model (used in the decoding step). Statistical phrase translation table usually has a higher coverage than a manually constructed phrase dictionary used in rule-based MT. So the impact of such context may be larger than in rule-based MT. This may explain why the word "drug" is translated correctly in more cases by Google than by Systran. For example, the fact that "drug" is used together with "traffic" will strongly influence the choice of the translation for "drug." This may be due to two factors. (1) If phrase-based SMT is used, "drug traffic" would likely be identified as a phrase, and it will be translated correctly as a whole. (2) Even if phrases are not used in SMT, or the given sequence of word is not identified as a phrase, the fact that a language model of the target language is used would be able to favor the sequence "trafic de stupéfiant" to "trafic de médicament," as the latter sequence is much less frequent in French than the former. In the second case, we see the impact of the translation of a word (traffic) on that of another word (drug). This principle will be later exploited in several studies in CLIR, which will be discussed in Section 2.4.2.

The utilization of phrase-based translation, or the immediate context, does not guarantee that the correct translation can always be selected. In the case of example 3—"drug research," the wrong translation "drogue" is selected in French, possibly because there are not enough parallel sentences containing "drug research" for it to be identified as a phrase. In this case, despite the use of the language model of the target language, the strong translation of the word "drug" by "drogue" in French cannot be overridden. On the other hand, the Chinese translation as "药物" happens to be correct. This case is somehow similar to the use of the default translation in Systran: in SMT, such "default" translation has a much stronger probability than other candidates. Similar reasons lead to the same selections of the translation words in examples 5 and 6.

Compared to rule-based MT, we can notice that the translations produced by SMT are not always syntactically correct. This is the case for the translation of "drug insurance"—"d'assurance médicaments" (a prepositional phrase). However, this syntactic difference between the original phrase (a noun phrase) and the translation (a prepositional phrase) does not affect CLIR, because only the keywords "assurance" and "médicament" will be used in IR processes. This aspect represents another strong difference between general MT and translation in CLIR that we described earlier.

2.2.3   Unknown Word

The case 4 also shows an example of unknown word—"Friedrich." This important concept has not been successfully translated in Chinese by either Systran or Google. Systran left it untranslated, while Google only translated part of it—"Fried" (as 弗里德). This partial translation may be due to several possible reasons: The corresponding Chinese proper name "弗里德赖希" may be incorrectly segmented into 弗里德 and 赖希 (which can translate the proper name "Rice") in parallel texts, or the proper name "Friedrich" is incorrectly decompounded in English. As a result, the translation model will suggest "弗里德" as a stronger translation word for "Friedrich" or for "Fried" than弗里德赖希. The translation of proper names is a difficult problem. When a proper name is involved in a query, it usually corresponds to an important concept. Its incorrect translation will usually have a great impact on the retrieval effectiveness. We will talk about this problem in more detail in Section 3.7.2.

All the examples that we have shown so far point to a number of potential problems when we blindly rely an off-the-shelve MT system for their translation.

1. The translation words selected can be wrong. This error will unavoidably affect the retrieval effectiveness. In rule-based MT systems, the errors are often related to the default translation word. In SMT, the use of a training parallel corpus on topics different from the given query could be a reason of it. For example, The query "Worldwide Oil Pipelines" is translated by Google as "Worldwide Oléoducs." The use of "Worldwide" in the translation is likely due to the use of general Web parallel documents (containing many occurrences of "Worldwide Web") for model training. A possible solution would be to train translation models specific for topic areas. This method is proposed in Hildebrand et al. (2005). But one has to determine in advance the set of topic areas.

2. Translation is limited to one per word, while there are multiple expressions for it in the target language. For example, both "drogue" and "stupéfiant" are correct French translations of "drug" in the sense of illegal substance, but both Systran and Google only choose "stupéfiant" in their translations of "drug traffic." Many relevant documents can use a different expression (e.g., "traffic de drogue," which is a commonly used term in French). These documents cannot be retrieved. It is thus desirable to include all the possible (correct) translation alternatives into the query translation so as to increase the recall. The restriction to one translation word per source word is unsuited to IR.

3. Translations provided by MT systems are limited to literal translations. MT systems do not suggest non-translation, but strongly related, words in the translation results. However, strongly related words are very useful in IR, even if they are not translation words. For example, it may be useful to "translate" the word "computer" by the French word "programme" even if the latter is not a literal translation of the former. This latter term may help retrieve other strongly related documents, which could be relevant.

4. Difficulty to translate unknown words, or out-of-vocabulary words (often referred to as OOV): users can request for many new events and use new terms in their queries that have

not been stored in dictionaries. A typical case is the translation of names of persons and organizations. In one of the examples we showed, a personal name is involved: "Friedreich." This name has been "translated" correctly from English to French (indeed, no translation is required in this case); but Systran has been unable to find a translation for it in Chinese, leaving it untranslated, while Google provided a partial translation. Translations for new technical terms can also be inappropriate. For example, the word "surfing" is usually translated as "冲浪" (surfing waves), but usually as "浏览" when it concerns web surfing. This second translation is widely recognized now. However, at the beginning of WWW, "Web surfing" in a query would have been translated as surfing waves in Chinese. Such situation constantly occurs when a new meaning is associated to a word, while its translation will take some time to follow. This case is not what we call OOV in the traditional sense. However, it concerns a sense that is not covered by the existing dictionary or translation models, and its correct translation is also unknown in reality. So, we also consider this case to be related to OOV.

Notice that the above problems are not specific to the approach of query translation using MT systems. The same problems may also occur using other translation approaches (e.g., using a dictionary). What is different in the latter case is that when we use open resources and tools, we can tailor them to the specific purpose of CLIR, which is difficult to do with off-the-shelve MT systems.

Another strong difference between MT and translation in CLIR is the role of syntactic structure. This aspect is very important in MT, but marginally important in IR. Through the steps of Systran translation, we can see that much effort has been put on determining the correct syntactic structure of the source and target texts. Similar efforts have been made in SMT (although in a different manner). Part of these efforts is useful in helping select correct translation words as in an expression such as "drug insurance." However, the final syntactic structure of the translated query does not have much impact on the retrieval results. For example, if the translation word is correctly selected, whether the translation is "d'assurance medicaments," "assurance de médicament" or "médicament assurance" (with an incorrect syntactic structure) will not lead to very different retrieval results in most IR systems.

MT systems have been used in a number of CLIR experiments. The results vary much according to the test collections, the MT systems used as well as the language pairs: from 50% to 100% of that of the monolingual IR (with manually translated queries). Typically, for well-studied languages such as European languages, the current MT systems perform quite well. One can usually achieve CLIR effectiveness equivalent to between 80% and 100% of the monolingual IR effectiveness. However, for resource-poor languages (e.g., Indonesian) or between very different languages (between English and Chinese), the CLIR effectiveness using an MT system can be as low as 50%

of the monolingual IR (Adriani and Wahyu, 2005) (Kwok 1999). Such effectiveness is not much better than a simple utilization of a bilingual dictionary.

The differences between MT and query translation we mentioned above open the door for a simpler translation tool tailored for CLIR, which ignores the analyses that do not impact the quality of query translation, but tries to produce a translation result with wider coverage. The next section describes one such attempt.

2.3.   OPEN THE BOX OF MT

Ideally, one would like to have a costume-tuned MT system for the specific purpose of CLIR. Technically, this would be feasible, but still not available for our use. What is the most desirable is to remove the limitation to one translation per word. Kwok (1999) observed the inappropriateness of this limitation for CLIR in an early experiment on English-Chinese CLIR. He proposed the use of multiple translations instead of a single final translation provided by the MT system—TransPerfect. This MT system allowed him to output an intermediate translation result with multiple translations for each word. For example, the query "building information super highway" can be translated as follows:

建筑[建立] 消息[知识/报告] 上等的[表面的]　公路[大道/直接的途径]

where [. . .] contains alternative translations for each word. In fact, this intermediate result is produced by nothing more than a simple dictionary lookup. As we can see, more translations for each source word can be included. However, for this particular query, the MT system failed to suggest the following correct translation words for the source words in this query:
building－建设, information－信息, 资讯, super－超级, highway－高速公路.

The addition of more, inappropriate, translation words will make the translation even worse. The quality of the dictionary is clearly the main source of the problem. In his experiments, Kwok only obtained a retrieval effectiveness of CLIR equivalent to 55% of that of monolingual retrieval, which is not better than using one translation per source word by the MT system. However, from the above example, one can see that the ineffectiveness of the approach stems from the quality of the bilingual dictionary of the MT system. It is possible that the approach with an MT system of better quality can produce a higher effectiveness. This is confirmed by several other studies, for example Xu and Weischedel (2000).

When Kwok exploited the intermediate translation results, basically, he exploited the bilingual dictionary provided by the MT system. So a legitimate question is whether the MT system can be replaced by a machine-readable bilingual dictionary?

What we could lose is the capability of MT system to select translation words using certain contextual information and linguistic structure. However, as we saw, this capability is not fully exploited in all the MT systems. On the other hand, a selection process can also be made in a dictionary-based query translation, as we will see in the next section. So, the capability of selecting translation words can be gained with a simpler approach than a full MT system.

Another strong motivation to use a bilingual dictionary is its high availability. Indeed, machine-readable bilingual dictionaries exist for many pairs of languages, while high-quality MT systems do not.

The above reasons have motivated extensive utilizations of bilingual dictionaries in CLIR. In the next section, we will examine some typical approaches to query translation using bilingual dictionaries.

2.4. DICTIONARY-BASED TRANSLATION FOR CLIR

In a bilingual dictionary, each word or phrase in the source language is translated into the target language by one, and often several words or phrases.

Dictionaries are organized according to different principles. For CLIR, dictionaries are usually considered as a word list, together with their translations. For example, a segment of the LDC[4] English-Chinese dictionary is as follows:

AIDS	/艾滋病/爱滋病/
data	/材料/资料/事实/数据/基准/
prevention	/阻碍/防止/妨碍/预防/预防法/
problem	/问题/难题/疑问/习题/作图题/将军/课题/困难/难题是/
structure	/构造/构成/结构/组织/化学构造/石理/纹路/构造物/建筑物/建造物/

For French-English, below is a fragment from FreeDict[5]:

accent:	accent, stress
accentuer:	accent, accentuate, stress
accepter:	accept, receive, take, take in

In some other dictionaries, such as Collins dictionaries,[6] in addition to translation words/phrases, examples and definitions are also provided. For example, below is a segment of the translation of the word "drug" into French:

drug

(n):

(=medicine) médicament *m*

$\rightarrow$ This drug is prescribed to treat hay fever.

---

[4]http://www.ldc.upenn.edu/.

[5]http://freedict.com/.

[6]http://www.harpercollins.co.uk/about-harpercollins/Pages/about-us.aspx.

They need food and drugs: Ils ont besoin de nourriture et de médicaments.

> to be on drugs: [patient] être sous médication

(=narcotics) drogue *f*

> → Cocaine is a highly additive drug.

> to take drugs: se droguer

> → She was sure Leo was taking drugs.

> to be on drugs: se droguer

> He's on drugs.: Il se drogue.

The additional information provided in the dictionary (such as examples and definitions) could be used to help select more appropriate translations in the context. For example the approach of Lesk (1986) could be adapted for this purpose. The approach proposed by Lesk aims at determining the correct word sense using a dictionary containing definitions of words. Given a text (or a text fragment) containing an ambiguous word, the word sense whose definition is the most similar (using a cosine similarity) to the given text is selected. This method can be adapted to select the translation word whose definition (or example) is the most similar to the given query. Suppose a query on "drug prescribed for diabetes," the first translation "medicament" can be considered to be more similar to the query due to the presence of the word "prescribed" in the example "This drug is prescribed to treat hay fever."

However, such additional information is usually unavailable in most dictionaries used for CLIR experiments. Therefore, in this section, we will assume a simple form of dictionary—a translation word list.

2.4.1 Basic Approaches

Dictionaries are usually used for a word-by-word translation. Given a source-language word in a query, the first question one should ask is what translation is appropriate and should be chosen. As we stated earlier, unfortunately, many available bilingual dictionaries do not contain useful information to help select the appropriate translation words or expressions. In such a situation, two basic approaches have been proposed in the early studies:

1.   Using all the translations for each query word;
2.   Using the first translation listed in the dictionary.

The first approach is motivated by the fact that when all the translations are used, one can include all the possible expressions in the target language and obtain a query expansion effect. Indeed, using the English–Chinese dictionary from the LDC, one can obtain both correct translations for "AIDS" in Chinese: 艾滋病and爱滋病. However, this is done at the cost of introducing incorrect translations due to ambiguities. In fact, many words in a language have more than one meaning. The multiple translations of a word included in a dictionary usually correspond to its different meanings. By including all the translations, some of them that are inappropriate (thus wrong) for the context will also be included. For example, when the French word "accent" is translated into both "accent" and "stress" (which have different meanings) using FreeDict, one of the translations is incorrect depending on the situation. The fact that the incorrect translation is included in the query translation will lead to retrieving irrelevant documents concerning the incorrect meaning of the original word. As a result, the increase in recall is often gained at the cost of decrease in precision. Overall, this simple strategy is not effective.

The second strategy—using the first translation listed—is motivated by the fact that the first translation is often the most frequently used (this is, of course, dependent on the way in which the dictionary is organized). In doing so, one expects to have a higher chance to obtain the appropriate translation. Similarly, when frequency information is available, one can also choose the most frequent translation word. This strategy is similar to the idea of using the default translation in MT when no additional information is available. However, this assumption on the organization of the dictionary is not true is many dictionaries. For example, FreeDict provides the following French translations for the English word "access"[7]:

access: attaque, accéder, intelligence, entrée, accès

The first translation "attaque" (attack) is certainly not the most used translation for "access." Therefore, this strategy will fail with this dictionary.

For the dictionaries that are organized according to the frequency of translation words and phrases, this strategy can help filter out some incorrect and rarely used translations. However, it also prevents one from having multiple translations for the same word. For instance, even if one is able to identify the most frequent translation word "爱滋病" for "AIDS" (assuming that the frequency information is available), "艾滋病" is also used in many cases to mean the same thing. Limiting to one translation will prevent us from retrieving documents using the second term.

Experiments using both strategies have shown relatively low retrieval effectiveness, often in the range of 50–60% of that of monolingual retrieval (Ballesteros and Croft, 1997; Oard and Dorr, 1996). These results show that the above simplistic methods are insufficient.

2.4.2   The Term Weighting Problem

We can observe several problems in the above simple translation methods. Term weighting in both documents and queries is an important aspect in IR. Using the first naïve approach—to include

---

[7]Some of these translations are incorrect (attaque) and the correct one (accès) is wrongly accentuated (accés), which is corrected in this example.

all the translation candidates into the translation, we can observe that the terms that have more translations in the dictionary will be artificially enhanced, in comparison to terms that have fewer translations. For example, imagine an English query containing "data structure" and assume that we use the LDC English–Chinese dictionary. The first term has 5 translations, while the second term has 10 translations. Putting them together into a bag of words would result in the following translated query:

/材料/资料/事实/数据/基准/
/构造/构成/结构/组织/化学构造/石理/纹路/构造物/建筑物/建造物/

This query will implicitly attribute higher importance to the meaning of "structure" than to "data." Similarly, for a query on "problem of AIDS prevention," the translation will contain far more translation words for "problem" than for "AIDS." So, the translations of "problem" will dominate those of "AIDS." We see that the very fact that more translations are included in the dictionary for a term directly has a significant impact on the relative importance of the term in the query. However, this is not intended in the original query.

A simple solution to this problem is to perform a normalization of the term weights for translations per source term, i.e., the weight of a translation becomes $1/n$, where n is the number of translation for the source term. Xu and Weischedel (2005) showed that this simple normalization approach can effectively correct the unbalanced weighting between different sets of translation terms. They have improved the CLIR effectiveness (MAP) from about 50% of that of the monolingual IR to 70–80%.

Pirkola et al. (1998, 2003) proposes a structured query translation approach: different translations for the same word are considered to be synonyms. They are combined using the #syn() operator in INQUERY system (Broglio et al., 1994), which considers a set of terms as synonyms and tries to accumulate the matches in the set. For the above example, one would create the following translated query:

#sum(#syn(材料, 资料, 事实, 数据, 基准),

    #syn(构造, 构成, 结构, 组织, 化学构造, 石理, 纹路, 构造物,

        建筑物, 建造物))

The combination of the translation terms in such a structure also implicitly changes the weighting of the translation terms within the query and allows to better balance the relative importance of the two parts of the query ("data" and "structure"). Pirkola showed that this structured translation is more appropriate than the flat translations: they achieved an effectiveness of 77% of that of monolingual IR, compared to 52% using a flat translation strategy.

Notice that another commonly used weighting factor is the idf factor. By multiplying the idf weight of a translation term, frequent terms in the target language will be assigned a lower importance than less frequent terms. This contributes in increasing the CLIR effectiveness. However, this is a "standard" method and is used on translations produced by almost all the methods.

2.4.3   Coverage of the Dictionary

The quality of translation is strongly dependent on the quality of the dictionary, including the correctness and the completeness (or coverage) of the translations included. However, it is difficult to directly test the impact, as the quality of the dictionary involves different aspects and it is difficult to measure. Nevertheless, Xu and Weischedel (2005) have tested one of the aspects: the coverage of source terms by the dictionary. They tried to reduce a dictionary to different sizes (in terms of the source-language entries) by keeping the most frequent portion and examined the impact of this on retrieval effectiveness. They found that when the size of the dictionary increases, the CLIR effectiveness also increases up to a certain point. For English–Chinese CLIR, the increase stops when the size of the dictionary reaches 10,000 entries (i.e. including the translations for the 10,000 most frequent English terms). On English–Arabic CLIR, similar phenomenon is observed. This simulation shows that once the dictionary reaches certain coverage of frequent source-language words, the further increase of the size of the dictionary will not necessarily improve more the CLIR effectiveness. This simulation should be interpreted in its context, though: The test queries in TREC only use quite frequent English terms, and these terms can be correctly covered by a dictionary of reasonable size. However, if users are allowed to submit free queries as on the Web, one would expect that further increase of the size of dictionary beyond 10,000 could have a larger impact on CLIR effectiveness.

Another aspect that has not been tested in the simulation is the completeness of the target-language translations. A dictionary can provide more or less translations in the target language. Although no test has been performed to simulate the effect of the completeness of the translations, one could reasonably expect that a dictionary providing more complete translations could lead to a better CLIR effectiveness in general, than a dictionary containing fewer translations. However, when the number of translations increases, there is also a higher danger to introduce noise and rarely used terms into the translation.

Taking both aspects into account, we can expect that a higher coverage in both source-language and target-language words could increase the CLIR effectiveness. However, the increase is likely not monotonic with the increase in the coverage of the dictionary. Another aspect not investigated so far is the correctness of the translations included in the dictionary. For example, the translations of "access" by "attaque" and "intelligence" in FreeDict are questionable. In summary, more studies are required to see exactly how one can measure the quality of the dictionary for CLIR tasks and how this quality can impact on CLIR effectiveness.

2.4.4 Translation Ambiguity

The experiments using the simplistic approaches based on dictionaries have shown several potential problems (Ballesteros and Croft, 1997):

- Specialized terms may not be contained in a dictionary, and its translation may not be up-to-date (e.g., the translation of "surfing" for Web surfing);
- Translations stored in a dictionary could be inherently ambiguous (e.g., the translations of "drug");
- Phrases may not be translated correctly if they are not covered by the dictionary (e.g., "pomme de terre" in French).

Among these problems, Hull and Grefenstette (1996) identified ambiguity and missing translation as the two main problems in using dictionaries.

The problem of missing translations can be addressed by automatically mining additional translation relations. We leave this problem to Section 3.7. In the next section, we will describe approaches to deal with the ambiguity problem—the selection of the most appropriate translation words.

2.4.5 Selection of Translation Words

Let us assume for now that the correct translation of the word is included in the dictionary, together with several other candidates (for the same or different meanings). The key problem is to be able to select the correct (or the most suitable) translation(s) among all the candidates. This is a way to solve the ambiguity problem. The selection of the first (or the most frequent) translation is a first step in this direction. However, the most frequent translation may fail to fit the context of the query. For instance, the English word "bedroom" is possibly the most common translation of the French word "chambre." However, this translation is inappropriate in expressions such as "musique de chambre" (chamber music) and "chambre de commerce" (chamber of commerce). A better solution is to make the selection context-dependent, i.e. according to the query or to the other words that co-occur in the query.

Grefenstette (1999) observed that the correct translation words usually have a higher frequency of co-occurrences with other translation words. Therefore, he proposed to use the frequency of co-occurrences of translation words to perform the selection. Let us use the example of "data access" to illustrate the idea. Suppose we use FreeDict, which provides the following translations for these words:

data: donnée, matériau, data
access: attaque, accéder, intelligence, entrée, accès

If we examine the combinations of translations for both words, we will have the following set:

(donnée, attaque), (donnée, accéder), …, (donnée, accès), …, (data, accès).

It is unlikely that the incorrect translations (e.g., (donnée attaque)) could have a high frequency of co-occurrences in French texts. The combination that has the highest frequency of co-occurrences would likely be (donnée accès), which is the correct translation in this case.

Similar ideas have been incorporated in more sophisticated methods (Gao et al., 2001; Liu et al., 2005; Adriani and van Rijsbergen, 2000). In these approaches, one defines a measure of *cohesion* between a set of translation words to select translation words. The goal is to select a set of best translation terms, one per source-language word, that are the most cohesive (i.e., tend to appear together in the target language). The cohesion measure is defined using a measure of similarity $\text{sim}(t_1, t_2)$ between two words t_1 and t_2. Gao et al. (2001) used point-wise mutual information between the terms as the similarity measure, Adriani and van Rijsbergen (2000) used Dice similarity, while Liu et al. (2005) used mutual information. The cohesion is then defined as the sum of similarity between all the translation words selected for the whole query. The selection criterion can be formulated as follows:

$$\arg\max_{T_Q} \text{Cohesion}(T_Q) = \arg\max_{T_Q} \sum_{T_{ti} \in T_Q} \sum_{T_{tj} \in T_Q \land t_j \neq t_i} \text{sim}(T_{t_i}, T_{t_j})$$

where T_Q is a set of translation words formed by one translation per source-language word, and $T_{t_i} \in T_Q$ is a translation candidate for term t_i. As the selection of the best translation for a term depends on the selection of those of other terms, Gao et al. proposed a greedy process for the selection: in each round of the process, the best translation for one source term is determined while the translations for other terms remain unchanged, and the process continues until no change is observed in the selection. In the experiments of both Gao et al. (2001) and Liu et al. (2005), this strategy has shown to be able to successfully select better translation terms, and the CLIR effectiveness obtained is significantly higher than the simple approaches without selection described previously. In the experiments of Gao et al. (2001), the effectiveness on TREC-9 English–Chinese CLIR is even higher than that of Chinese monolingual IR.

A similar approach is used by Seo et al. (2005). The difference with the method of Gao et al. (2001) is that Seo et al. explicitly enumerate all the combinations of translation terms for a query, and the combination with the highest score is selected. As in Gao et al. (2001), Seo et al. also found such a selection of best translation terms useful, and this generally improved the CLIR effectiveness.

Various variants of the above approach have been used. For example, Maeda et al. (2000) used the term co-occurrence statistics in the target language to select the translation candidates whose combination has a similarity higher than a threshold. This allowed them to select multiple translation words per source word.

One can also consider word order in the combinations of the translation words Jang et al. (1999): instead of considering all the combinations of translations terms, one can limit the combinations of the translation words for consecutive words in the query only. For example, for a sequence of three words "automobile air pollution," only the relationships between *automobile-air* and *air-pollution* are considered. However, this constraint does not always lead to selecting the best word combinations and useful non-consecutive combinations (e.g., *automobile-pollution*) could be left out. In an approach proposed for monolingual IR, which could also be used for translation selection, Gao et al. (2004a) proposed a statistical parsing process to select the strongest connections (dependencies) among query words, which does not necessarily follow the word order in the query. However, for typical short queries, it is still unclear whether such a selection of dependency relations is always better than considering all the combinations. Indeed, Metzler and Croft (2005) have successfully integrated unselected dependencies within a query: they integrate both ordered and unordered dependencies between adjacent words in a Markov Random Field model and demonstrated that this model outperforms significantly the model which does not consider term dependencies.

Syntactic structures of the query can also be considered in translation selection (Gao and Nie, 2006): for example, one can favor cohesion between the translations of the words that form a noun phrase in the query. The syntactic constraint also showed some improvement in CLIR effectiveness. However, the improvement is less than when statistical relations are considered. This is likely due to the fact that, on the one hand, the syntactic structure we can recognize is not always correct, and on the other hand, contextual word does not need to be in some specific syntactic structures to be useful. This latter aspect has been evidenced in IR in many studies.

All the above approaches used a static similarity or cohesion measure between terms. Monz and Dorr (2005) and Zhou et al. (2008) believe that the cohesion measure is a dynamic decision process, in which the similarity between different terms acts collectively to "elect" the best translation candidates. They construct a graph to link the translation candidates for different source terms and allow the links to dynamically vote for the best candidates. Several strategies have been used, including selecting the translations that represent the highest *centrality* in the graph, the highest *indegree* or *authority* measure, or the highest probability after random walks, and so on. However, Monz and Dorr (2005) did not provide a comparison of the iterative selection to the static selection method. In Zhou et al. (2008) a comparison was made; but the results did not demonstrate that the dynamic process contributed much to improve over a statistic selection process. A possible reason for this is that the dynamic process is typically useful when there are a large number of nodes, and one tries to use the mutual reinforcements between nodes to select some of the strongest connections. In the case of short queries, as the number of nodes is limited, the dynamic process will often be unable to produce a reliable probability distribution (or weighting) much different from the initial distribution, if one does not want to suffer from the effect of query drift. So, the advantage of such a dynamic selection for query translation over a static selection process could be limited.

One common practice we observe in the above approaches (except Maeda et al., 2000) is to limit to one best translation per source word. This restriction prevents one from expanding the query by more alternative expressions. To solve this problem, Maeda et al. (2000) proposed to replace the *argmax* operator on cohesion by a threshold: all the translation candidates whose cohesion with other translation terms is higher than a threshold are kept. This extension points to an interesting direction to produce a greater effect of query expansion. More investigations are needed to see its impact and how far we can go in this direction.

2.4.6   Other Related Approaches

2.4.6.1 Phrase-Based and Structured Query Translation

In addition to entries of single words, dictionaries can also contain entries for compound terms or phrases. For example, a French-English dictionary may contain the following compound entry:

base de données: database

pomme de terre: potato

It has been observed that phrases should not be discomposed and translated word by word using their constituents. A typical case is "pomme de terre" (potato) in French, whose word-by-word translation would be "apple," "soil/earth," which is incorrect. To solve this problem, several studies have proposed to use phrase translation (Ballesteros and Croft, 1997; Ballesteros and Croft, 1998; Hull and Grefenstette, 1996; Meng et al., 2001). A common approach is to use phrase translation in priority: phrases are first translated as a whole if their translations are included in the dictionary; then the remaining words are translated word by word. This approach avoids the above problem of inappropriate translations for non-compositional phrases. The experiments showed that the CLIR effectiveness can be much improved using such a two-stage translation process. However, this approach requires a dictionary with phrases and their translations. In general, such a dictionary only covers a limited number of phrases and translations. One should also look for methods to identify such phrases and their translations automatically.

The studies on phrase-based machine translation could seem appropriate to this end (Kohen et al., 2003). However, one has to notice an important difference between the requirement for phrase-based translation and that in general MT: a phrase identified in Kohen et al. (2003) is a consecutive sequence of words. In IR, we have observed that a word may be connected to distant words, as shown in Gao et al. (2004a). On the other hand, phrases such as "there is," that are important in MT, are not important in CLIR, as they and their translation will likely be treated as stopwords and will not have any impact on CLIR. Although phrase-based SMT has improved the translation quality measured in BLEU, it is not clear that this improvement can also materialize in CLIR effectiveness. The differences between general MT and CLIR rather suggest that the phrase translation required in CLIR is different from that in general MT. These problems require further investigations in the future.

2.4.6.2   Using Multilingual Thesauri

A bilingual dictionary can be viewed as a simplified and poor bilingual thesaurus in which only translation relationships are created between equivalent terms in two languages. A true multilingual thesaurus contains richer relationships between terms, such as *is-a, part-of, related-to*, and so on. In fact, such multilingual thesauri have been widely used in the first attempts to MLIR in library science (Oard and Dorr, 1996). Thesauri have been constructed for different languages: Greek, French, English, German, and so on. In many cases, the thesauri are used to help the user select the appropriate controlled vocabulary to include in their queries. The multilingual dimension of the thesauri provides a simple means to translate the controlled vocabulary into other languages. The inclusion of richer relationships between terms also allows the user to extend the query by related terms (e.g., more general or more specific terms). However, in most cases, the selection of the related terms was left to the user, so was the selection of a proper (Boolean) structure to combine different terms in the query. On automatic use of such resources, Gilarranz et al. (1996) has used a multilingual thesaurus—EuroWordnet, to help perform conceptual text retrieval. In more recent experiments, Ruiz et al. (2000) and Gey and Jiang (2000) have also tested CLIR approaches based on a conceptual interlingua or multilingual thesaurus: terms in each language is translated into a standard interlingual representation, or into terms in other languages. The approaches used are similar to those used in the earlier experiments. The experiments suggest that if the thesaurus in use corresponds well to the concepts in a particular area (e.g., in medicine), the above approach can be highly useful. However, in general IR, one is often faced with several problems in such an approach:

- First, the manual construction of such a resource is very expensive in human resources.
- Second, a manually constructed thesaurus may not contain all the concepts and terms expressing the concepts, even if we allocate all the necessary human resources to construct it. One reason is the evolving nature of concepts and terms—new terms are constantly created to describe new concepts and technologies. A manual construction can never follow the pace of such a quick evolution. This is particularly true for the IT-related terminology. Another critical aspect is that new terms and proper names are frequently used in modern Web searches, and one cannot expect to have a thesaurus or a name translation dictionary[8]

---

[8]Some name translation dictionaries, for example, for Chinese-English, are provided by LDC.

to cover all such terms. Therefore, the concepts (or terms) in a query may fail to be translated.

- Third, it is not obvious that a strong semantic relation that the experts decide to include in a thesaurus or selected by the user is truly useful for IR. This situation is similar to the use of a thesaurus in monolingual IR (Voorhees, 1994). For example, a strongly related (translation) term determined manually may appear in no or few documents. The inclusion of such terms may not be useful. In addition, a seemingly strongly related term may be ambiguous, leading to retrieving documents for a different meaning.

- Finally, the seemingly semantically unrelated translation terms may be very useful for IR. For example, in monolingual IR, it is difficult to foresee a semantic relationship between the term "Olympic games" and "hotel price" and to store it in a thesaurus in advance. However, when we look for the information about "hotel price" in a city where Olympic Games are to be held, the two terms become strongly related. A document about "hotel price during the period of Olympic Games" may be particularly relevant. This illustrates the fact that useful relationships between terms are not limited to those recognized by human experts. It may often be the case that simple co-occurring terms in documents provide useful indication to other pieces of relevant information. This is the very basis of using term co-occurrences in IR, which proved to be more useful than human-crafted semantic relations (Cao et al., 2005; Mandala et al., 1998). In CLIR, we have similar situations.

The above observations have motivated attempts to create a bilingual dictionary or similarity thesaurus automatically from parallel or comparable texts (Braschler and Schäuble, 2001) using less strict criteria. We will describe some of such work in the next chapter.

· · · ·

CHAPTER 3

Translation Based on Parallel and Comparable Corpora

Parallel texts are texts with their translations in another language. More and more parallel texts are becoming publicly available. These texts are rich resources that contain translation relations between texts, sentences, phrases, and words. Many approaches have been proposed to extract such translation relations from them. In this chapter, we will describe some representative approaches used in both SMT and CLIR based on parallel texts. In fact, many approaches to CLIR based on parallel texts exploit the same translation models proposed for SMT. There are indeed much in common between query translation and MT. However, as we have already seen, they are also different in some respects.

Comparable texts are texts that are topically similar without being parallel (i.e., translations one for another). Such texts are more available than parallel texts. Although it is difficult to exploit comparable texts extensively for MT tasks, it is possible to use them for CLIR due to the less strict requirement in CLIR.

In this chapter, we will first describe the processing of parallel corpora in the MT community. Then we will describe the ways to use resulting translation models in CLIR. Several alternative approaches to CLIR using parallel and comparable corpora will also be described. Finally, we will describe approaches to automatically mine parallel texts and translation relations from the Web.

3.1 PARALLEL CORPORA

Parallel corpora have been widely exploited for the purposes of translation since the 1990s. A typical example is the Canadian Hansard[1]—a parallel corpus containing the debates of the Canadian parliament in French and English. A segment of it appears in Figure 3.1.

Similar parallel corpora also exist in other languages. For example, the European parliament produces parallel corpora (EuroParl) between all the official European languages (English, French,

---

[1] http://www.parl.gc.ca/common/chamber.asp?Language=E.

English	French
Securing Our Energy Future	**Assurer notre avenir énergétique**
Energy is vitally important to our country. Our geography and climate mean that Canadians depend on affordable and reliable energy. The development of our rich energy resources is an important source of wealth and Canadian jobs.	L'énergie est une ressource vitale dans ce pays. Pour des raisons de géographie et de climat, les Canadiens doivent avoir accès à des sources d'énergie abordables et fiables. La mise en valeur de nos richesses énergétiques contribue grandement à la prospérité et à la création d'emplois pour les Canadiennes et les Canadiens.
Our Government will support the development of cleaner energy sources. The natural gas that lies beneath Canada's North represents both an untapped source of clean fuel and an unequalled avenue to creating economic opportunities for northern people. Our Government will reduce regulatory and other barriers to extend the pipeline network into the North.	Notre gouvernement encouragera le développement d'énergies propres. Les nappes de gaz naturel dans le Nord du Canada représentent à la fois une source inexploitée de combustible propre et une voie incomparable vers de nouvelles perspectives économiques pour la population du Nord. Notre gouvernement réduira les obstacles en matière de réglementation et autres afin d'étendre le réseau de gazoducs dans le Nord.
These measures will bring jobs to northern Canada and create employment across the country, just as they will bring new energy supplies to markets in southern Canada and throughout the world. Economic development in Canada's North, led by a new stand-alone agency, is a key element of our Northern Strategy.	Ces mesures seront porteuses d'emplois autant dans le Nord que dans le reste du pays. Elles procureront en même temps de nouvelles sources d'approvisionnement en énergie aux marchés du Sud du Canada et du monde entier. Le développement économique dans le Nord canadien sera confié à un nouvel organisme distinct dans le cadre de notre Stratégie pour le Nord.
Nuclear energy is a proven technology, capable of reliable, large-scale output. In Canada and around the world, energy authorities are investing in nuclear power to meet both energy security and climate change goals. Our Government will ensure that Canada's regulatory framework is ready to respond should the provinces choose to advance new nuclear projects.	Le nucléaire constitue une technologie éprouvée et fiable pour produire une énergie abondante. Au Canada et ailleurs dans le monde, les autorités énergétiques investissent dans le nucléaire pour atteindre leurs objectifs en matière de sécurité énergétique et de lutte contre les changements climatiques. Notre gouvernement veillera à ce que le Canada ait une réglementation efficace afin d'encadrer d'éventuels projets nucléaires provinciaux.

FIGURE 3.1: An excerpt of the Hansard parallel corpus.

English	Chinese
RESOLVED that with effect from the establishment of the Government of the Hong Kong Special Administrative Region on 1 July 1997-	議決通過由 1997 年 7 月 1 日香港特別行政區政府成立之日起—
1.　　　　there shall be established a fund called the Land Fund;	1．　　　　設立一基金，稱為土地基金；
2.　　　　the Land Fund shall receive and hold all of the assets, including all accounts receivable, net of expenses, transferred, upon the establishment of the Government of the Hong Kong Special Administrative Region, from the Hong Kong Special Administrative Region Government Land Fund established by a Declaration of Trust of the Hong Kong Special Administrative Region Government Land Fund Trust made on 13 August 1986 to the Government of the Hong Kong Special Administrative Region and which have become part of the general revenue in accordance with section 3 of the Ordinance and the provisions of the Declaration of Trust of the Hong Kong Special Administrative Region Government Land Fund Trust;	2．　　　　土地基金須接收和持有藉於 1986 年 8 月 13 日訂立的香港特別行政區政府土地基金信託的《信託聲明書》而設立的香港特別行政區政府土地基金在香港特別行政區政府成立時，按照本條例第 3 條及香港特別行政區政府土地基金信託的《信託聲明書》的條文，在扣除開支後移交予香港特別行政區政府，並已成為政府一般收入的一部分的所有資產，包括所有應收帳項；

FIGURE 3.2: An excerpt of the Hong Kong Hansard parallel corpus.

German, Spanish, and so on)[2]. The official documents from the Hong Kong Legislative Council[3] are also bilingual in Chinese-English (see Figure 3.2).

The raw parallel texts are aligned at the text level—a text is aligned to its translation. This alignment level is too coarse to be directly usable for translation purposes. Most approaches that exploit parallel corpora at a finer level try first to align parallel texts at paragraph and sentence level,

[2] http://www.europarl.europa.eu/guide/search/docsearch_en.htm.

[3] http://www.legco.gov.hk/general/english/counmtg/yr00-04/mtg_0304.htm.

then to align them at word/phrase level through the training of translation models—as we described in the last chapter. Here, we will describe sentence alignments methods.

3.2   PARAGRAPH/SENTENCE ALIGNMENT

High-quality translations usually follow the same paragraph and sentence order: a paragraph or sentence that appears first in the source language is usually translated first in the target language. This general phenomenon can be observed in the examples shown above. It is used in most paragraph/sentence alignment algorithms. Here, we describe in some detail the algorithm of Gale and Church (1993).

Gale and Church first aligned parallel texts into paragraphs using special formatting markers in the texts. In their case, they worked on parallel documents in English–French–German from the Union Bank of Switzerland—UBS. This first step can be performed quite easily and reliably, as the corpus contains clear paragraph boundary markers. It is then assumed that paragraphs are aligned 1-to-1. In the second step, sentences within the corresponding paragraphs are aligned. For sentence alignment, one can no longer assume that sentences are aligned 1 to 1. One source sentence can be translated into several sentences (1-n alignment); several sentences can be translated into one sentence (n-1 alignment). A source sentence can be omitted in the translation process (1-0 alignment) or a sentence can be added in the translation (0-1 alignment). To deal with these problems, in addition to the general order of sentences between the source and target languages, Gale and Church also used the general observation that long sentences are usually translated by long sentences, and short sentences by short sentences, and they proposed to use dynamic programming to determine the best alignments between sentences.

The sentence alignment problem can be formulated as follows: given a pair of texts (or paragraphs) T_1 and T_2 in two languages, we assume that they can be segmented into sentences. Consecutive sentences in a text can be grouped into a passage, and there may also be empty passages. A successful alignment between the two texts means that each passage in one text is aligned with a passage in another text, and that there is no crossing alignment between passages. Then the problem is to find a set of alignments between passages such that

$$\arg\max_A P(A \mid T_1, T_2) = \arg\max_A \prod_{(L_1 \leftrightarrow L_2) \in A} P(L_1 \leftrightarrow L_2 \mid T_1, T_2)$$

where $(L_1 \leftrightarrow L_2)$ means that two passages L_1 and L_2 in T_1 and T_2 are aligned. It is further assumed that the alignment between two passages is independent from the context in which they appear.

Therefore:

$$\arg\max_{A} \prod_{(L_1 \leftrightarrow L_2) \in A} P(L_1 \leftrightarrow L_2 \,|\, T_1, T_2)$$

$$= \arg\min_{A} \sum_{(L_1 \leftrightarrow L_2) \in A} -\log P(L_1 \leftrightarrow L_2 \,|\, L_1, L_2)$$

Two classes of approaches are used to determine $P(L_1 \leftrightarrow L_2 \,|\, L_1, L_2)$: based on sentence length or based on lexical clues. In the approaches of the first class, it is assumed that this probability only depends on the lengths of the passages, which we denote by l_1 and l_2. Furthermore, it is assumed in (Gale and Church, 1993) that this is only dependent on a function $\delta(l_1, l_2)$ which estimates a length ratio between l_1 and l_2. Then the above equation is approximated by:

$$\arg\min_{A} \sum_{(L_1 \leftrightarrow L_2) \in A} -\log P(L_1 \leftrightarrow L_2 \,|\, l_1, l_2)$$

$$= \arg\min_{A} \sum_{(L_1 \leftrightarrow L_2) \in A} -\log P(L_1 \leftrightarrow L_2 \,|\, \delta(l_1, l_2))$$

Using Bayes rule, we have:

$$P(L_1 \leftrightarrow L_2 \,|\, \delta(l_1, l_2)) = \frac{P(\delta(l_1, l_2) \,|\, L_1 \leftrightarrow L_2) P(L_1 \leftrightarrow L_2)}{P(\delta(l_1, l_2))}$$

where $P(\delta(l_1, l_2))$ is a constant that we can ignore.

It is further assumed that $\delta(l_1, l_2)$ follows a normal distribution with a mean of c and variance of σ^2. Using a set of manually aligned sentences, Gale and Church found that c for French–English and German–English is, respectively, 1.1 and 1.06, and σ^2 is, respectively, 7.3 and 5.6. The following normalization transforms it to a standard normal distribution (with 0 mean and 1 derivation):

$$\delta(l_1, l_2) = \frac{l_2 - l_1 c}{\sqrt{l_1 \sigma^2}}$$

Then $P(\delta(l_1, l_2) \,|\, L_1 \leftrightarrow L_2)$ is determined as follows:

$$P(\delta(l_1, l_2) \,|\, L_1 \leftrightarrow L_2) = 2 \times (1 - P(|\delta(l_1, l_2)|))$$

The prior $P(L_1 \leftrightarrow L_2)$ depends on the type of alignment (1-1, 1-0, etc.). A set of training data is used to determine such probabilities, which are shown in Table 3.1:

TABLE 3.1: Alignment prior.	
CATEGORY	**PROBABILITY**
1-1	0.89
1-0 or 0-1	0.0099
2-1 or 1-2	0.089
2-2	0.011

To find the best alignment sequence A, dynamic programming with the following distance function can be used:

$$D(i,j) = \min \begin{cases} D(i,j-1) + d(0,1) \\ D(i-1,j) + d(1,0) \\ D(i-1,j-1) + d(1,1) \\ D(i-1,j-2) + d(1,2) \\ D(i-2,j-1) + d(2,1) \\ D(i-2,j-2) + d(2,2) \end{cases}$$

where $d(m,n)$ is measured by $-\log P(L_1 \leftrightarrow L_2 \mid l_1, l_2)$, in which L_1 and L_2 are passages containing respectively the last m and n sentences ($0 \leq m,n \leq 2$) in the two languages.

Sentence length can be measured in characters or in words (Brown et al., 1991). Gale and Church found the character-based length performs slightly better than word-based length on the UBS corpus.

For languages with large similarity such as English–French, *cognates* can also be used to enhance sentence alignment. Cognates designate words with the same or similar root in different languages. For example, the word "information" in English, French and German, the word "información" in Spanish and "informazioni" in Italian all have the same root *inform*. They are considered as cognates. It is assumed in Simard et al. (1992) that if we observe more cognates in the two candidate sentences, then there is a higher chance that they are aligned. The length-based distance measure is augmented by the number of corresponding cognates in their alignment algorithm as follows:

$$S_{cog} = \frac{p_T(c \mid n)}{p_R(c \mid n)} \times p(L_1 \leftrightarrow L_2 \mid \delta(l_1, l_2))$$

where $p_T(c \mid n)$ and $p_R(c \mid n)$ denote, respectively, the probability of aligned sentences and random sentences of length n to have c cognates. It turns out that this additional criterion can improve sentence alignment.

One can extend the above length-based alignment algorithms by incorporating more linguistic resources. For example, Kay and Röscheisen (1988) proposed the use of a dictionary to provide lexical clues to help sentence alignment. Between linguistically more different languages such as English and Chinese, lexical clues can be helpful. Wu (1994) augmented the length-based alignment algorithm by a dictionary, and found that this can improve sentence alignment between Chinese and English. The idea is similar to the use of cognates: the score of alignment is increased if we observe that the two candidate sentences contain many mutual translations. Wu used a small dictionary containing a set of corpus-dependent translations for words such as "Thursday—星期四," which appear frequently in the corpus. Larger dictionaries can also be used here.

3.3   UTILIZATION OF TRANSLATION MODELS IN CLIR

Once a parallel corpus is sentence-aligned, statistical translation models can be trained on it, as we described in Chapter 2.

Translation models developed for MT can be directly used in CLIR. Among different translation models, IBM model 1 is the most used in CLIR. Recall that in this model, no word order is considered during word alignment (or model training). As a result, a word that appears in a sentence can be translated by any of the words in the aligned sentence in another language. From an MT point of view, this possible translation is not sufficiently precise and higher-level models (e.g., IBM model 4) are preferred.

From a CLIR point of view, the loose translation constraint we impose during the model training process is not necessarily a disadvantage.

- Word order is not (yet) an important criterion to consider in IR. Most of the current approaches are based on independent words (bag of words). That is, a query can well match a document in which words are in a different order. For query translation, the most important is the selection of translation words, but not the order in which they are put in the translation.
- One may argue that the consideration of word order (and other criteria used in higher level translation models) can help determine more precise translations. This is because the additional criteria considered can further restrain the translation relationships between words in parallel sentences. This is true. However, one also has to consider another important factor in IR—the query expansion effect. By allowing looser translation relations between words

in parallel sentences, we can indeed naturally extend the strict translation relations to words that co-occur in the aligned sentence. As a result, a word can be translated not only by its literal translation(s), but also by the words that co-occur in the aligned sentences. This is indeed a query expansion process. Conceptually, it is equivalent of this as performing a precise translation (by the literal translation(s)), then expanding the translation by words that co-occur often in the same target-language sentences. This query expansion effect is generally desirable in IR.

In summary, although more sophisticated translation models can produce more precise translations (which enhance precision), we lose in coverage of related terms (which is related to recall). They are thus not necessarily more advantageous for CLIR.

In our subsequent description, we will focus the use of IBM model 1 in CLIR. We will assume that a translation model (IBM model 1) has been trained on a parallel corpus and we have a function $t(f|e)$ (and/or $t(e|f)$) that provides the translation probability between a source word e and a target word f. We will see how such a translation model can be used for CLIR.

A number of studies have been carried out to test the effectiveness of using translation models for CLIR, mainly, for query translation. The Hansard corpus has been used in many studies for CLIR. Here, we describe in more detail the experiments reported in Nie et al. (1998) for English–French CLIR (i.e., using English queries to retrieve French documents).

The Hansard parallel corpus used in this study contains 7 year's debates of the Canadian parliament, amounting to several dozens of millions of words in each language. The Hansard corpus is first processed to transform each word into its standard citation form before the translation model is trained. For example, "donné" and "donnée" are both transformed into the infinitive verb form "donner." This transformation was found to be slightly better than a standard stemming. Stopwords are also removed in both languages. Then an IBM model 1 is trained, resulting in a translation probability function $t(f|e)$.

Several other approaches to query translation have been compared to the translation model in this study: with a bilingual dictionary and with two MT systems (Logos and Systran). The experiments are performed on TREC-6 CLIR test collection (Schäuble and Sheridan, 1997) using vector space model with tf*idf weighting. This collection contains 141K to 250K documents in English, French, and German, with 25 test queries.

Using a small bilingual dictionary—Ergane, which contains less than 8000 words in each language, with the simple approach that includes all the translation words, the CLIR effectiveness (MAP) is about 50% of that of monolingual effectiveness (0.3731). This corresponds to the typical figure for this approach. Using Logos and Systran to translate queries, the MAP is respectively 0.2866 (76.8% of monolingual IR) and 0.2763 (74.1%). Using the translation models, they selected the top N translation words f with the highest translation probabilities for the whole query, which is:

$$P(f \mid Q_E) = \sum_{e \in Q_E} t(f \mid e) P(e \mid Q_E)$$

It is further assumed that $P(e \mid Q_E)$ in this equation is the same for every word e in Q_E. Therefore, the above equation is simplified to: $P(f \mid Q_E) \propto \sum_{e \in Q_E} t(f \mid e)$.

By keeping only the N strongest translation words, much translation noise with low translation probabilities can be filtered out. In addition to the translation probability, the corpus statistics about word usage, i.e., idf values, are also combined, leading to the following weight of the term:

$$w(f, Q_E) = \sum_{e \in Q_E} t(f \mid e) \times \log \frac{\mid C_F \mid}{n_f}$$

where $\mid C_F \mid$ is the number of documents in the French collection and n_f the number of documents containing the term f.

Table 3.2 shows the effectiveness with different N:

TABLE 3.2: CLIR effectiveness using a statistical translation model of Hansard (Nie et al., 1998).	
NUMBER N OF TRANSLATION WORDS	**MAP (%MONOLINGUAL IR)**
10	0.2546 (68.24%)
20	0.2635 (70.62%)
30	0.2660 (71.30%)
40	0.2664 (71.40%)
50	0.2671 (71.59%)
100	0.2506 (67.14%)

The above results show that the translation model can produce retrieval effectiveness higher than the simple approaches based on dictionary, but slightly lower than that with the MT systems, especially when N is set between 30 and 50. By inspecting the translation results, it is observed that the translation model is unable to distinguish between specific translation terms and general or common terms in the translation. In many cases, common words such as "prendre" (take), "donner" (give), and "pouvoir" (can/power) are suggested as strong translation words for many queries. These words are not included in the French stoplist, but do not have a specific meaning in a query. Below is an example of query and its translation by the translation model, where the numbers are the translation probabilities $P(f \mid Q_E)$:

Query #1 Reasons for controversy surrounding Waldheim's World War II actions.

```
affaire=0.069960
waldheim=0.067383
guerre=0.062125
raison=0.048319
ii=0.047925
monde=0.043656
controverse=0.038537
entourer=0.036864
mesure=0.022972
mondial=0.019244
prendre=0.018364
second=0.015948
suite=0.013105
action=0.011012
susciter=0.006899
donner=0.006639
pouvoir=0.006223
cause=0.005515
```

The reason for the inclusion of common terms in the translation is that these common words have a high frequency of co-occurrences with many source language (English) words in the parallel texts. Therefore, a relatively strong translation probability is assigned to them for many source language words. As a simple sum is used to produce the final translation probability for the whole query, these common words often appear among the top translation candidates for the query. One could argue that we can extend the stoplist to include such common words, so that they will not be proposed as translation candidates. Indeed, this could solve the problem of some such words; but there are many other common words that we cannot include in the stoplist. For example, the French word "donner," which could also represent the word "donnée" with the meaning of "data" (as in "base de données"—database), cannot be included in the stoplist. In addition, even with an extended stop-list, the same phenomenon still remains for other (possibly less) common words.

Notice that in addition to the translation probability, the idf value of the words is also used. It is expected that the common words have a smaller idf value than other words, thus their final weights will be smaller. Despite this, the inclusion of common words in the translated query, even at a very small value, can disorient the search process towards documents containing such words, which is not desirable.

Another possible solution to this problem is to reinforce the weights of other translation words, which could be suggested by a bilingual dictionary. For example, one may expect that a bilingual dictionary would store "affaire" as a translation of "affair," "guerre" as a translation of "war," but the common words such as "prendre" will not be suggested by the dictionary as translation words for the query (notice that stopwords have already been removed before translation). The fact that the weight of these specific translation words is increased will further reduce the impact of including some common words in the translated query.

In Nie et al. (1998), a simple method is used to implement the idea. A small bilingual dictionary (Ergane) is used to suggest translation words for the query. All these translation words are assigned a fixed default translation value, which is added to the translation probabilities produced by the statistical translation model. In their experiments, several default values are tested. Table 3.3 shows the impact of such a combination of translation models with the dictionary:

TABLE 3.3: Combining a translation model with a dictionary (Nie et al., 1998).

DEFAULT VALUE	NUMBER OF TRANSLATION WORDS					
	10	20	30	40	50	100
0.005	0.2671	0.2787	0.2812	0.2813	0.2829	0.2671
0.01	0.2755	0.2873	0.2891	0.2896	0.2906	0.2742
0.02	0.2873	0.2959	0.2962	0.2967	**0.2985**	0.2825
0.03	0.2811	0.2906	0.2898	0.2897	0.2904	0.2744
0.04	0.2751	0.2842	0.2827	0.2826	0.2831	0.2683
0.05	0.2687	0.2761	0.2729	0.2729	0.2730	0.2578

We can see that with a reasonable default value (0.01–0.03) for dictionary translations, this approach can largely increase the effectiveness of using the translation model alone, and it outperforms MT systems (Systran-0.2763 in MAP and Logos-0.2866 in MAP) in several cases: the highest effectiveness is 80.0% of the monolingual effectiveness. This result is very encouraging. It shows that for CLIR purposes, we do not need a sophisticated MT system. A statistical translation model automatically trained on a parallel corpus, supplemented with a bilingual dictionary, could provide an even better solution. This result is further confirmed by a number of studies later (e.g., Kraaij et al., 2003, which will be described later).

The combination of a statistical translation model with a bilingual dictionary is often used in CLIR. By such a combination, one may expect to benefit from the strength of each type of resource: the bilingual dictionary can suggest the usual translations for query words, while the statistical translation model can increase the coverage of translation and better tune the translation probability according to the parallel corpus.

Through inspection of the translations, we do observe inappropriate translations by the statistical translation model, especially when ambiguity is involved. This is the case for the following query (similar problem has also been observed with MT systems, see Section 2.2):

Query #3 What measures are being taken to stem international drug traffic?

```
médicament=0.110892
mesure=0.091091
international=0.086505
trafic=0.052353
drogue=0.041383
découler=0.024199
circulation=0.019576
pharmaceutique=0.018728
pouvoir=0.013451
prendre=0.012588
extérieur=0.011669
passer=0.007799
demander=0.007422
endiguer=0.006685
nouveau=0.006016
stupéfiant=0.005265
produit=0.004789
```

The term "drug" is translated into both the incorrect term "médicament" and the two correct ones—"drogue" and "stupéfiant." This is because the debates in the Canadian Hansard discuss about both the legal medication and illegal drug problems and the IBM model 1 only proposes translations word-by-word and ignores the context words in the query. This observation suggests that a disambiguation process can be added to select the correct translation words. A possible approach is similar to that used by Gao et al. (2001) and Liu et al. (2005), as we discussed in Section 2.4.2.

The above approach is typical in CLIR. Comparing with SMT, one can notice that only translation models are used, and the language model component in SMT is ignored. The language model component helps SMT to select more appropriate sequences of words in the target language. A question we should ask is whether a similar component should be added into a CLIR model to perform the selection of translation words. In fact, the previous studies (Gao et al., 2001; Liu et al., 2005) have already demonstrated that such a component could be very useful to query translation. The cohesion measure integrated in their models plays a similar role to the language model in SMT: the goal of both is to select the translation words that fit better in the target language. However, we also noticed some important differences between the cohesion measure and the traditional language model component: (1) The language model component only considers consecutive words, while the cohesion measure can span over distant words in a sentence. (2) The language model component considers functional words, while the functional words are usually considered as stopwords and are not included in the calculation of cohesion. These differences are intimately related to the different goals in general SMT and translation in CLIR: the goal in query translation is not the generation of a grammatically correct translation, but to help select the most appropriate translation terms without much regard to grammatical rules or word order. Therefore, one should use a component different from the traditional language model. The approach of Gao et al. (2001) and Liu et al. (2005) suggests that the component could be a cohesion measure between the translation words of the query. Let us denote it by *cohesion*(T_{Q_E}). Then a possible model that determines a set of translation words could be as follows:

$$P(T_{Q_E} \mid Q_E) = \text{cohesion}(T_{Q_e}) \times \prod_{f \in T_{Q_e}} \sum_{e \in Q_e} t(f \mid e) P(e \mid Q_e)$$

To our knowledge, this model has not been tested so far. Its effectiveness has yet to be demonstrated.

Besides the studies of Gao et al. (2001) and Liu et al. (2005), another work similar in spirit to the above model is Federico and Bertoldi (2002), in which, in addition to a word translation model, a target language model (n-gram model) is used to select among the *n* best translation words. It is shown that one can obtain significantly better results using a target language bigram model than with a target language unigram model. This result also suggests that the combination with a cohesion measure could be a promising avenue. However, a cohesion measure requires less strict word order than a bigram model, and it can be better suited to CLIR.

3.4   EMBEDDING TRANSLATION MODELS INTO CLIR MODELS

The approaches we described so far used a translation model as an external resource. The translation probabilities are considered as weights of terms, which are used in the subsequent monolingual IR process with various IR models. The typical schema of CLIR in two separate steps—first translation, then monolingual retrieval—can achieve reasonable effectiveness in most cases. However, the connection between the two steps is set manually. One may naturally ask the following question: would it be possible and beneficial to integrate both the translation step and the retrieval step within a uniform framework for CLIR? This is indeed possible and quite easy to achieve within the language modeling framework. In this section, we describe some attempts to develop language models for CLIR, which naturally integrate translation probabilities within the models.

Recall that the score of a document D to a query Q in language modeling can be estimated by cross-entropy as follows:

$$\text{Score}(D, Q) = \sum_{t_i \in V} P(t_i | \theta_Q) \log P(t_i | \theta_D)$$

where θ_Q and θ_D are, respectively, the language (unigram) model of the query and the document. For a document and a query in the same language, t_i takes value in the same vocabulary (V). When they are in different languages, we have to integrate a translation model in one of the language models. The integration of a translation model is often based on an IR model, called *translation IR model* (Berger and Lafferty, 1999), which was inspired by the translation model in MT, but originally proposed for monolingual IR. The basic idea of this model is to extend the document language model by incorporating relationships between terms, formulated as a "translation" probability $t(t_i | t_j)$ between two terms t_i and t_j of the same language:

$$P(t_i | \theta_D) = \sum_{t \in V} t(t_i | t_j) P_{ML}(t_j | \theta_D)$$

In comparison with the traditional language modeling approach, in which we only use $P(t_j | \theta_D)$ (usually smoothed with a collection model), the above model allows us to take into consideration the relationships between terms. In Berger and Lafferty (1999), the relationship between t_i and t_j

is estimated from a pseudo-parallel corpus created from a monolingual corpus as follows: each sentence is considered to be "parallel" to the paragraph containing it. Then a translation model (IBM model 1) is trained on it to obtain $t(t_i|t_j)$.

The above translation IR model can be naturally extended to CLIR, by training a true translation model $t(t_i|s_j)$ between words t_i and s_j in two languages. The translation model can be incorporated in both the document model and the query model.

(1) Integrating translation into query model (or query translation approach—QT)

The new query language model is defined as follows:

$$P(t_i \mid \theta_{Q_s}) = \sum_{s_j \in V_s} P(t_i \mid s_j, \theta_{Q_s}) P(s_j \mid \theta_{Q_s})$$

$$\approx \sum_{s_j \in V_s} t(t_i \mid s_j) P_{ML}(s_j \mid \theta_{Q_s})$$

where Q_s is a source-language query, t_i a target-language term, $t(t_i \mid s_j)$ is the translation probability from the source-language term s_j to the target-language term t_i, and θ_{Q_s} is the traditional query language model in the source language estimated by Maximum Likelihood (ML) estimation. The document score is then determined as follows:

$$score(Q_s, D_t) = \sum_{t_i \in V_t} P(t_i \mid \theta_{Q_s}) \log P(t_i \mid \theta_{D_t})$$

$$= \sum_{t_i \in V_t} \sum_{s_j \in V_s} t(t_i \mid s_j) P_{ML}(s_j \mid \theta_{Q_s}) \log P(t_i \mid \theta_{D_t})$$

Notice that the document model θ_{Q_t} in the target language should be properly smoothed as in monolingual IR. Kraaij et al. use Jelinek–Mercer smoothing, combining with the collection model.

As the translation model is noisy, one can select a subset of translation terms t_i to be considered by setting a threshold on $t(t_i|s_j)$, or by considering the n strongest translation candidates in the translation model. This selection process can filter out much translation noise.

(2) Integrating translation into document model (or document translation approach—DT)

Similarly, one can also estimate the following document model in the source language:

$$P(s_i \mid \theta_{D_t}) = \sum_{t_j \in V_t} P(s_i \mid t_j, \theta_{D_t}) P(t_j \mid \theta_{D_t})$$

$$\approx \sum_{t_j \in V_t} t(s_i \mid t_j) P(t_j \mid \theta_{D_t})$$

Then the document score can be determined as follows:

$$\text{score}(Q_s, D_t) = \sum_{s_i \in V_s} P(s_i | \theta_{Q_s}) \log P(s_i | \theta_{D_t})$$

$$= \sum_{s_i \in V_s} P_{\text{ML}}(s_i | \theta_{Q_s}) \log \sum_{t_j \in V_t} t(s_i | t_j) P(t_j | \theta_{D_t})$$

Kraaij et al. used translation models trained on parallel web pages mined automatically using PTMiner (see Section 3.7.1). The above approaches have been tested on the combined CLEF—2000, 2001, and 2002 test collections with 140 test queries. Table 3.4 shows the effectiveness for English–French (i.e., queries in English and documents in French), French–English, English–Italian, and Italian–English experiments. Several other methods are compared: monolingual IR, and query translation using the Systran MT system.

One can see that using both integrated QT and DT approaches, the effectiveness is higher than using the MT system. It achieves CLIR effectiveness equivalent to around 90% of the monolingual IR between English and French, and around 80% between English and Italian. This shows once again that translation models, when used in an appropriate manner, can outperform a high quality MT system.

Xu et al. (2001) and Xu and Weischedel (2005) used a similar approach. The translation models are built with GIZA++ on a parallel corpus of documents from the United Nations, or a

TABLE 3.4: Effectiveness of integrated CLIR model on CLEF test collections (Kraaij et al., 2003).

RUN	EN-FR	FR-EN	EN-IT	IT-EN
Monolingual	0.4233	0.4705	0.4542	0.4705
Systran MT	0.3478 (82.2%)	0.4043 (85.9%)	0.3060 (67.4%)	0.3249 (69.1%)
QT	0.3878 (91.6%)	**0.4194** (89.1%)	0.3519 (77.5%)	**0.3678** (78.2%)
DT	**0.3909** **(92.3%)**	0.4073 (86.6%)	**0.3728** (82.1%)	0.3547 (75.4%)

pseudo-parallel corpus generated by translating a TREC collection using an MT system (Systran or Language Weaver). The document language model is extended in the following manner:

$$P(s_i \mid \theta_{D_t}) = \lambda \sum_{t_j} t(s_i \mid t_j) P(t_j \mid \theta_{D_t}) + (1-\lambda) P_{ML}(s_i \mid \theta_{C_s})$$

where C_s is a general source-language collection, which is used to generate a background model. The above approach is slightly different from the one used in Kraaij et al. (2003): the source-language collection model θ_{C_s} is used to smooth the translated document model, while Kraaij et al. used a target-language collection model θ_{C_t} to smooth the untranslated document model. As in Kraaij et al. (2003), Xu et al. also showed that this method can produce excellent CLIR effectiveness, at the level of 90% of that of monolingual IR.

Another line of study is to extend the relevance model (Lavrenko and Croft, 2001) to CLIR. A relevance model R_Q for a query $Q = e_1 \ldots e_k$ is estimated by:

$$P(w \mid R_Q) \approx P(w \mid Q) = \frac{P(w, e_1 \ldots e_k)}{P(e_1 \ldots e_k)}$$

The original relevance model assumes w to be in the same language as $e_1 \ldots e_k$. When the model is extended to CLIR (Lavrenko et al., 2002), w is a target language word, while $e_1 \ldots e_k$ are terms in the source language query. $P(w, e_1 \ldots e_k)$ is estimated using a parallel corpus as follows:

Assume a set of parallel texts $\{E, C\} \in M$ in English and Chinese. For a given target language (Chinese) word w, $P(w, e_1 \ldots e_k)$ is estimated as follows:

$$P(w, e_1 \ldots e_k) = \sum_{\{E,C\} \in M} P(\{E,C\}) P(w \mid \theta_C) \prod_{i=1}^{k} P(e_i \mid \theta_E)$$

In their implementation, Lavrenko et al. (2002) assumed a uniform $P(\{E, C\})$. Therefore, we have

$$P(w, e_1 \ldots e_k) \propto \sum_{\{E,C\} \in M} P(w \mid \theta_C) \prod_{i=1}^{k} P(e_i \mid \theta_E)$$

The parallel corpora used in the experiments are the Hong Kong News parallel dataset, which contains 18,147 news stories in English and Chinese, and TDT pseudo-parallel texts containing 46,692 Chinese news articles and their translations produced by Systran. It turns out that the TDT parallel texts contributed more in the retrieval effectiveness than the Hong-Kong News parallel texts, mainly due to its larger size and wider coverage. In fact, this relevance model approach relies more on the use of pseudo-relevance feedback than a translation model per se. Indeed, no translation model is explicitly estimated and the set M of parallel texts is used to identify a subset of top-ranked documents that are used as pseudo-feedback documents for the estimation of the language model. From this perspective, this approach uses a coarser-grain translation relation than the approaches based on a translation model between terms. The coverage of the query topic by the parallel corpus is the most important factor for such an approach. This may explain why the larger TDT parallel corpus generated by the automatic Systran MT system has a larger impact on the CLIR effectiveness than the smaller set of parallel news articles.

The experimental results on TREC-9 English–Chinese test collection showed that the cross-language relevance model outperforms a traditional translation model, and it achieves an effectiveness equivalent to about 90% of the monolingual IR. However, this approach depends on some parameters such as the number of top-documents to be used as feedback documents. The fact that no fine-grained translation relations are extracted before hand also makes it difficult to further improve the approach. In addition, one also has to perform retrieval twice—one for identifying pseudo-feedback documents, and another for the real retrieval. Possibly due to all these reasons, this approach has not been followed later in other studies.

It is interesting to note that the cross-language relevance model, which exploits coarse-grain translation relationships, can compete with approaches that use fine-grain translation relationships. This shows once again that the translation quality (as seen in MT) is not the only concern in CLIR. The inclusion of related terms that help identify relevant documents is also important.

The models we described in this section all point to a promising direction: instead of using a translation tool or resource as a separate, external, resource to IR, one can integrate the translation component within a unified CLIR model. The experiments reported indicate that such an integrated approach could be advantageous compared to a separate translation. The main advantage of such integration is that it can make more appropriate use of the translations so that the translations can fit the IR purpose. However, the above approaches are still limited in trying to adapt the translation model toward IR: in fact, the translation models used are still trained by a tool (usually using GIZA++ toolkit) designed for a different goal from CLIR—to maximize the translation probability between two languages (including for functional words). Although a high-quality translation usually means high retrieval effectiveness in CLIR, as we stated earlier, a useful term for CLIR can also be a non-translation related term. The use of a less strict translation model—IBM model 1—can allow us to capture some of such related terms in the translation. However, this is more a side-effect than the expected goal of the translation model. In general, what we try to achieve in estimating a translation model for the purpose of general MT is to restrict the translations to the desired translation terms rather spreading them to related terms.

So a remaining question is whether it is more appropriate to design a training process with the explicit goal of maximizing the cross-language relevance rather than translation probability. In such a training process adapted to CLIR, the probability of related translation terms is increased because of their impact on the final CLIR effectiveness, while the translation probabilities of common or functional words are reduces because of their limited impact on CLIR. More specifically, instead to maximize the translation probabilities between aligned sentences in the training parallel corpus, one can try to relate the training process to the final measure, e.g. MAP in CLIR. This is, however, not an easy enterprise, as CLIR effectiveness is not a measure that we can easily model solely within the parallel corpus. More external criteria are involved (i.e., user's relevance judgments). Some recent studies have investigated the problem of parameter estimation within machine learning frameworks so as to maximize the final retrieval effectiveness, namely within the learning-to-rank paradigm (Liu, 2009). However, such approaches have not yet been used within the training process of translation models in CLIR. This is an area in which further research should be carried out.

Another area of research is the relationship between the parallel corpus and the final document collection on which search is performed. Ideally, one would want to have a parallel corpus in the same area as the searched document collection. However, this is often impossible. Therefore, in the previous studies, independent parallel corpora are used to estimate translation models. In general, one could expect that the translation determined through an independent parallel corpus, if it is large enough, can cover the usual translation terms. However, when we deal with documents and queries in a specific domain (e.g. medical domain), a more related parallel corpus would be required. This problem has been investigated in SMT: (Hildebrand et al., 2005) tried to determine a portion of the parallel corpus related to the texts to be translated in order to train a more specific translation model for the texts. A similar approach could be used in CLIR: One can select an appropriate parallel corpus for CLIR in a given area. This is an interesting problem to be investigated in the future.

3.5   ALTERNATIVE APPROACHES USING PARALLEL CORPORA

Although most studies for CLIR based on parallel corpora use translation models developed for SMT, several other alternatives have also been investigated specifically for CLIR. In this section, we describe some of them.

3.5.1   Exploiting a Parallel Corpus by Pseudo-Relevance Feedback

Yang et al. (Carbonell et al., 1997; Yang et al., 1998) used the traditional pseudo-relevance feedback approach to exploit a parallel corpus, without training a translation model: The source-language query is first used to retrieve a set of source-language documents from the parallel corpus (on the

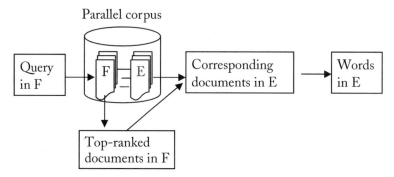

FIGURE 3.3: Exploiting a parallel corpus by pseudo-relevance feedback.

source-language side). The corresponding target-language documents are then used to extract a set of terms in the target language, which is considered to be the "translation" of the original query. This method works in the same spirit as cross-language relevance model we described in Section 3.4. Figure 3.3 illustrates the process of this approach, using a French query to generate an English "translation."

However, the experiments did not show that this approach can achieve comparable effectiveness to translation models.

Davis and Dunning (1995) used a similar approach: They extract a set of "significant" terms from the 100 Spanish documents in a parallel corpus corresponding to the English documents retrieved with the original English query and used them as a "translation" of the query. Their experiments on TREC-4 data showed a large loss in MAP of about 95% compared to monolingual IR.

In Davis and Ogden (1997), the parallel corpus is used in a different way—to select the best translation candidates among those suggested by a bilingual dictionary. The candidate that allows retrieving a similar set of documents in the parallel corpus to that retrieved by the original term is considered to be the best choice.

The above approaches only exploit a coarse-grain alignment of the parallel corpus at text level. While they are robust, they do not allow us to exploit the finer-grain alignment at word or phrase level. When such a finer-grain alignment is possible, it is advantageous to do it rather than remaining on the text level. However, these approaches are suitable to comparable texts when no or insufficient parallel corpus is available.

3.5.2   Using Latent Semantic Indexing (LSI)

LSI (Deerwester et al., 1990) aims to create a new representation space to represent the "latent semantic" dimensions of documents and queries. The dimensions are those that correspond to the largest singular values of the document-term matrix. More specifically, given a term-document matrix X, it is decomposed by Singular Value Decomposition (SVD) into three components:

$$X = TSD'$$

where T and D are left and right singular vector matrices, and S is a diagonal matrix of singular values. Then a clean-up process is carried out to cut off the weakest singular values, which are assumed to correspond to noise in the representation. This transforms the original matrix and its transformation to the following form, which keeps the k strongest singular values:

$$X = T_k S_k D_k'$$

It is equivalent to think that a new representation space of k dimension is created, and documents are mapped into it as $S_k D_k'$. Given a query Q indexed by terms in the initial term space, it can also be mapped into the new representation space as $T_k'Q_k$. Then the score of the documents to the query can be determined according to their cosine similarity in the new space.

The LSI approach has been tested on several small collections for monolingual IR (Deerwester et al., 1990), and it has been shown to outperform the traditional vector space model. The observed advantage of LSI is that it is capable to map strongly related terms into the same dimension of the new representation space (synonymous terms), while making difference between different meanings of ambiguous terms according to their contexts of utilization (polysemious terms).

LSI has been used later on larger TREC collections (Dumais, 1994), but the superiority of LSI was less clear than on small collections—the LSI model performed at equal effectiveness level to traditional vector space models (Harman, 1994). In addition, the high computation cost for computing SVD has been an obstacle to its utilization on very large collections.

The new representation space created by LSI can also be bilingual or multilingual, and documents and queries in different languages can be mapped into such a bilingual or multilingual space. This provides a way to perform CLIR. This approach exploits a parallel corpus as follows: the aligned texts in two languages are combined, producing an artificial document containing terms in both languages. From such a term-document matrix, the new latent semantic space is created by SVD. Different from the monolingual case, this SVD will allow one to map terms in both languages into the new unified space, thereby achieving an implicit translation. With such an LSI approach, no explicit query or document translation is necessary. The score of a document to a query in a different language can be calculated by the cosine similarity of their vectors in the new space as before.

In the CLIR experiments reported in Dumais et al. (1996, 1997) on some small test collections, the CLIR effectiveness was shown to be excellent—close to that of the monolingual IR. However, the test collections are not standard ones and it is difficult to compare directly with other approaches. In Mori et al. (2001), the above method was used on a standard English–Japanese test collection in the NTCIR-2 experiments. The practical problem they encountered is the computation complexity of SVD. Mori et al. solved this problem by dividing the set of parallel texts into several subsets, and SVD is performed on each subset separately to create subspaces. Although, this allowed them to create an LSI representation, the division of the training parallel corpus into subsets gave rise to the problems of unknown words in the sub-LSI spaces. As a consequence, many terms cannot be mapped into the new subspaces. The expected advantage of creating a unified latent space is much reduced.

The experiments of Mori et al. showed an important problem with LSI: the high computation complexity of SVD. So, only relatively small parallel corpora can be used for LSI. But as other studies showed, the CLIR effectiveness is strongly related to the size of the parallel corpus. Until this problem is correctly solved, the interests for using LSI in CLIR remain rather theoretical.

In terms of retrieval effectiveness, the experiments performed so far have not demonstrated that LSI is competitive compared to other approaches on large test collections. In Mori et al. (2001), the CLIR effectiveness is lower than the effectiveness obtained by the other participants in the same TREC and NTCIR experiments using explicit translation. Similar observation has been made in Lu et al. (2004), in which the LSI method was tested with a set of pseudo-parallel texts (newspaper articles on the same topics).

Besides the practical problem of computation, there is also a more fundamental question: SVD tries to determine the best k singular values for representing the original document-term matrix, so that the square error of the representation is minimized. While this minimization makes sense for many applications, it is not obvious that the same minimization captures well the real semantics of documents and terms, and can allow retrieving relevant documents.

3.5.3   Using Comparable Corpora

Parallel corpora are not always available for many languages pairs. It is however easier to obtain *comparable corpora* in which texts in two languages concern the same topics without being strictly parallel (i.e., translation one for another). For example, many newswire articles in different languages talk about the same events everyday. Although they are not parallel, one may expect that the same important elements are described in them in different languages. Their contents are thus *comparable*. This strategy has been used in Sheridan and Ballerini (1996) to collect a set of comparable texts.

Given the more noisy nature of comparable texts, it is inappropriate to exploit them using the same strategy as for parallel texts. For example, it would be inappropriate to train a fine-grained translation model SMT from a comparable corpus. A more robust and coarse-grain approach should be used. Several studies have been carried out using comparable corpora for CLIR (Sheridan and Ballerini, 1996; Braschler and Schäuble, 2000; Moulinier and Molina-Salgado, 2003; Franz et al., 1999). In general, one tries to determine a cross-language similarity between terms in two languages according to their co-occurrences within the corresponding comparable texts. The more two terms co-occur in the comparable texts simultaneously, the more they are assumed to be similar in meaning. One can use a large variety of similarity measures: cosine similarity, mutual information, and so on. Notice that the construction of such a cross-language similarity thesaurus is very similar to that of monolingual similarity thesaurus (Crouch and Yang, 1992), with the only exception that co-occurrences are found for a pair of terms in two different languages. Once a cross-language similarity thesaurus is built, query translation becomes a process very similar to query expansion in monolingual IR: each query term is replaced by the set of (weighted) similar terms in another language. Again, the idf factor of terms in the target language can be used to make a difference between frequent and infrequent terms.

At a first glance, it may seem risky to use such comparable corpora for CLIR. However, the exploitation is consistent with the principle of pseudo-relevance feedback and co-occurrence analysis in monolingual IR: we are interested in determining terms that are used to describe the same (or similar) event in another language. These terms likely represent the same concepts or the concepts that are frequently related to the query topic. So, in the context of CLIR, the strategy is reasonable.

Nevertheless, the similarity thesaurus created in such a way can be very noisy: terms with different meanings can happen to co-occur often in the comparable texts. In particular, many newswire articles do not necessarily concentrate on one event, but may also talk about other background and related events, which can be different in different languages. It is thus better to try to extract the cross-language similarity relations from portions of comparable texts that have stronger correspondence.

The approach used in Franz et al. (1999) goes in this direction. It tries to refine the roughly aligned comparable texts into better aligned segments. More specifically, each text is segmented into passages (e.g., 50 words). Within a certain time window (e.g., the newspaper published in the same day), one tries to determine the possible "parallel" passages by using an initial translation resource (e.g., a bilingual dictionary) as follows: the passage is first translated into another language in order to retrieve the passage in another language with the highest score. This latter passage is considered to be "parallel" to the former. This approach may result in a set of corresponding passages of higher quality, and the translation model (or similarity measure) built from them could be better.

In the above approach, the identification of corresponding passages is helped by a bilingual dictionary. One can naturally extend this approach by using a statistical translation model to determine the degree of parallelism between passages. It is also possible to use the presence of clues such as proper names (if the languages are similar) and other named entities (Braschler and Schäuble, 2000) to help determine if two passages may correspond. These approaches exploit similar strategies to cognate-based sentence alignment.

Whatever the refinement is used, the noisy nature of comparable corpora still remains, and this makes it risky to train a statistical translation model in the same way as from parallel corpora. One has to use a more robust similarity measure. In general, such similarity relations are less precise than the translation relations from a parallel corpus. This difference has been observed in the previous experiments performed on the same test collections in TREC and CLEF (Braschler and Schäuble, 2000): In general, translation relations from a parallel corpus perform better than cross-language similarity relations. Nevertheless, when no better resources are available for a pair of languages, the approach based on comparable corpora is shown to be very useful.

3.6   DISCUSSIONS ON CLIR METHODS AND RESOURCES

Approaches described so far in this chapter can be distinguished according to the resources they use: parallel texts or comparable texts. Parallel texts are more and more available, making it possible to extract translation relations from them. However, when no or limited parallel corpus is available, comparable corpora can be used to estimate less precise cross-language similarity relations.

On the approaches proposed in the literature, one can distinguish two categories:

- Statistical translation model: this family of approaches is based on parallel texts, and relies heavily on the strict parallelism between sentences in two languages in order to extract fine-grain translation relations between words or phrases.
- IR approaches: this family of approaches relies on a loose correspondence between comparable texts. Bilingual term similarity, instead of translation relations, is extracted. Typically, we extend the co-occurrence analysis to a comparable corpus, or use the pseudo-relevance feedback mechanism to determine related terms in another language (as in Yang et al., 1998).

Both types of resources and approaches have been proven to be useful in the experiments. However, overall, one can observe that parallel texts can lead to better translation relations than comparable texts, and an exploitation using statistical translation models performs better than that using cross-language term similarity.

The approaches used for query translation has much in common with SMT. The recent progress in SMT also suggests interesting future development for query translation. In particular, phrase-based translation approaches have become the state of the art in SMT, while these approaches have not yet been widely investigated in CLIR.

On the other hand, when we adopt approaches from SMT, one also has to keep in mind the differences between SMT and query translation. These differences suggest that a distinct translation model could be built specifically for query translation. The training process of such a translation model should target the objective of identifying a set of terms capable of retrieving relevant documents in another language. This objective is different from the alignment probability or BLEU score used in MT. The construction of such specific translation models for CLIR is an interesting area of future research.

3.7   MINING FOR TRANSLATION RESOURCES AND RELATIONS

The previous sections made it clear that CLIR heavily relies on bilingual resources, be they bilingual dictionaries, parallel, or comparable texts. These resources, however, may be unavailable, insufficient, or incomplete. It is thus desirable to compile such resources automatically.

Fortunately, there are more and more publicly available texts and parallel texts, which contain rich translation relations. This section describes several attempts to mine translation resources and relations automatically.

3.7.1   Mining for Parallel Texts

A critical aspect of the approaches based on parallel corpora is the requirement to have such large corpora. Although there are several large parallel corpora for European languages, no large parallel corpus exist for many other languages. Fortunately, the Web has emerged more and more as a large repository of multilingual texts. In many cases, Web sites are bilingual or multilingual. For example, the Canadian Government maintains their Web pages in both English and French. Wikipedia is another example of multilingual site. The Web has become a truly mixed corpus with potentially a large number of parallel texts. The problem is to extract them.

The first attempts to mine parallel texts from the Web go back to Resnik (1998) and Nie et al. (1999). While Resnik (1998) only showed that it is possible to mine parallel texts from the Web automatically, Nie et al. (1999) also showed that the mined texts can be successfully used for CLIR and the effectiveness is competitive to a high quality MT system. Several other studies followed and parallel corpora are constructed for different language pairs—between English and French, Italian, German, Chinese, Japanese, Arabic, and so on (e.g. Nagata et al., 2001; Resnik and Smith, 2003).

In general, the mining process exploits the general organization of bilingual (or multilingual) websites. When two sets of parallel texts are to be provided on a website, webmasters usually organize them in a way that can facilitate the navigation between the parallel texts by human users, as well as their maintenance. Some of the commonly used organization strategies are as follows (Huang and Tilley, 2001):

1. Linking each text to its counterpart in another language.

   In this organization, each text contains a link pointing to its counterpart in another language.

2. Creating two parallel structures in both languages.

   It is assumed in this organization that we have indeed two parallel sub websites, each for a language. The documents in the two languages are separately stored in each sub website.

3. Naming convention.

   It is often observed that parallel Web pages are often given the same name, with a small segment to indicate the language. For example, if an English version of the text is named "report_en.htm," its French equivalent would likely be "report_fr.htm." Although there are exceptions, such a naming schema is generally used.

The above widely used organization methods provide heuristics to the automatic mining process.

In STRAND, Resnik (1998) used the heuristics that parallel Web pages are often referenced from the same home page, with anchor texts indicating their languages. For example, the home page "http://www.nserc-crsng.gc.ca/" (see Figure 3.4) references two other pages in French and English, respectively with anchor texts "English" and "French": "www.nserc-crsng.gc.ca/index_eng.asp" and "www.nserc-crsng.gc.ca/index_fra.asp." STRAND extracts these Web pages and considers them to be parallel.

In Nie et al. (1999) similar observation has been made and exploited. More heuristics are used to recognize more parallel texts as follows:

1. Parallel texts can reference each other, and usually with an anchor text indicating the language. For example, a French Web page can link to its English version with an anchor text "English version," and vice versa. This heuristic is used to retrieve a set of parallel Web pages in order to determine if a website could be bilingual.

2. Parallel texts often possess similar URLs. Usually, the only difference between the URLs of parallel pages lies in a segment which indicates the language. The segment can be a part of the file name such as "index_en.html" and "index_fr.html," or a directory name in URLs as in ".../en/index.html" vs. ".../fr/index.html." This heuristic is used to determine possible pairs of parallel pages.

3. In addition, parallel web pages should describe the same content, thus leading to similar lengths (or a length ratio close to the normal length ratio between the two languages).

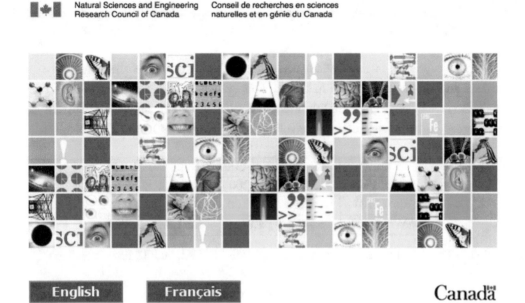

FIGURE 3.4: A snapshot of the home page "http://www.nserc-crsng.gc.ca/," which contains references to an English page and a French page.

This criterion is used to filter out obvious non-parallel pairs with too large differences in length.

The above heuristics are incorporated into the PTMiner system (Chen and Nie, 2000), which works as follows:

- First, candidate web sites are determined using the first heuristics: a website where one can find parallel web pages corresponding to the first criterion is considered to be a candidate site. To do this, a search engine (AltaVista) is used: a query is issued to retrieve documents in one language (e.g., French), but containing an anchor text indicating another language (e.g., "english," "English version," "version anglaise," "en anglais," etc.), and vice versa. The websites of these documents are identified as candidate parallel websites.
- Then a crawling process is used to mine as many web pages as possible from the candidate sites. This crawling is performed because many web pages on these sites are not indexed by the search engine.
- The name similarity between URLs in two languages (second heuristic) was used to match quickly a Web page to its possible equivalent in another language.

- Finally, the length similarity (heuristic 3) is used to confirm if the two pages determined can be parallel.

The above process is largely language-independent, except for the language-dependent anchor texts and language segments in URLs. This system has been used to mine parallel Web pages between several languages: English–French, English–German, English–Italian and English–Chinese. Figure 3.5 below summarizes the volume of the corpora mined in 2000.

	EN-FR	EN-GE	EN-IT	EN-CH
# Text Pairs	18,807	10,200	8,504	14,820
Size (MB)	174/198	77/100	50/68	74/51
# Words (M)	6.7/7.1	1.8/1.8	1.2/1.3	9.2/9.9

FIGURE 3.5: The size of the parallel corpora mined from the Web by PTMiner (Kraaij et al., 2003).

The corpora have been used to build statistical translation models and then used for query translation in CLIR. Figure 3.6 shows the results of the first experiments for English–French CLIR using vector space model (Nie et al., 1999).

	TREC-6		TREC-7	
	FR-EN	EN-FR	FR-EN	EN-FR
Monolingual	0.2895	0.3686	0.3202	0.2764
MT (Systran)	0.3098 (107.0%)	0.2727 (74.0%)	0.3293 (102.8%)	0.2327 (84.2%)
Hansard + Dict	0.2560 (88.4%)	0.3053 (82.8%)	0.3245 (101.3%)	0.2649 (95.8%)
Web + Dict	0.2590 (89.5%)	0.3041 (82.5%)	0.2610 (81.5%)	0.2296 (83.1%)

FIGURE 3.6: Comparison of translations models trained with parallel Web pages and other methods.

Queries are translated using respectively Systran, translation models trained on the Canadian Hansard (Hansard model) and translation models trained on parallel Web pages (Web models). In the last two cases, a dictionary is used to enhance the translation models as described in Section 3.3. The table shows the best results we can obtain using different default translation value assigned to those suggested by the dictionary (0.03 for TREC-6 and 0.005-0.01 for TREC-7).

The results for TREC-6 show that the corpus mined automatically from the Web can lead to CLIR effectiveness close to that with the Hansard models. We notice a larger difference with

Web models on TREC-7. This difference can be explained by the fact that TREC-7 queries contain more named entities, in particular, names of countries. The Web translation model seems to have difficulties to translate them correctly. For example, "Sudan" is translated in French not only as "Soudan," but also as "Singapour," "Royaume unis," etc. with quite high probabilities. The translations for "Swiss" also include "United Kingdoms," "Canada," "Uzbekistan," "Ukraine," and "Turkey" among the top 25 candidates. An explanation to this phenomenon is that the Web documents mined contain lists of countries. Due to the simple preprocessing on Web documents, a list is taken together as forming a "sentence." This leads to the alignment between different countries during the model (IBM model 1) training process.

Despite this fact, the global effectiveness using Web models is close to that with Hansard models and Systran.

Notice also that the above experiments use vector space model with tf*idf weighting. The translation models are not tightly integrated within the retrieval model. In Section 3.4, we described the approach proposed in Kraaij et al. (2003) exploiting the same Web models, but within the language modeling framework. The results obtained in this latter study showed that the corpora mined from the Web can outperform Systran. Therefore, with a proper exploitation and integration of the Web models, we can obtain better retrieval effectiveness, competitive to the use of an MT system.

The experiments on mining parallel texts have been very successful for languages active on the Web, in particular, between English and another language. Parallel texts mined in this way can be used not only for query translation in CLIR, but also for SMT. Indeed, the SMT systems of Google already exploit the large amount of parallel Web documents that can be mined automatically. For languages less active on the Web such as Arabic, Thai, and Indian languages, the success is more limited. Kadri and Nie (2006) tried to adapt the PTMiner system to mine English-Arabic parallel web pages in 2004. However, only a small number of pages have been found and the resulting CLIR effectiveness is well below that obtained with a bilingual dictionary. It should be noted, however, that the difficulty for less active languages tends to be reduced, as more and more documents for these languages appear on the Web. For example, between 2000 and 2008, the increase of the number of documents in Arabic on the Internet is estimated at 1,545.2% by InternetWorldStats[4] while the increase for English is 218.4% for the same period of time. This rapid increase makes it possible to mine large parallel corpora for this pair of languages in the near future.

3.7.2   Transliteration

Missing translation is an important problem in CLIR (Hull and Grefenstette 1996). There are two cases of missing translation:

---

[4] http://www.internetworldstats.com/stats7.htm.

1. The source term is unknown (the OOV problem);
2. The source term is known, but the appropriate translation is missing.

The first category of problems often concern proper names—names of persons, organizations, places, and so on. When such a term appears in a query, it usually corresponds to an important part of the information need. Failure to translate it would result in low retrieval effectiveness. In languages with similar writing system (e.g., English, French), proper names are often written in the same way without change. There is no need to perform a specific translation. For example, if the proper name "Waldheim" in a French query is unknown, it can be simply left untranslated in an English translation without altering the retrieval effectiveness. In some cases, slight transformations may be necessary. For example, the French name "Bérégovoy" can be written in English as either "Bérégovoy" or "Beregovoy." However, such a transformation is quite straightforward.

For very different languages (e.g., between English and Asian languages), the fact that a proper name is untranslated will be very problematic. It cannot be expected that the translations of all proper names are stored in a dictionary, or extracted in a translation model. Many proper names are unknown. Automatic translation methods for proper names are thus necessary.

We observe that many proper names are translated into another language by pronunciation, which we call *transliteration*. For example, *Mao Tze-tung* or *Mao Zedong* - 毛泽东, *Yahoo* - 雅虎, *Elizabeth Taylor* - 伊丽莎白·泰勒. Automatic transliteration of proper names addresses this special case of translation.

The general approach to transliteration can be summarized into the following steps (Knight and Graehl, 1998; Gao et al., 2004b; Cao et al., 2007b):

1. The proper name in the source language is first transformed into its corresponding phonetic sequence (pronunciation).
2. The phonetic sequence of the source language is transformed into a phonetic sequence of the target language. This transformation is necessary because some sounds in a language may not exist in another language (e.g., the pronunciation for "Ra" does not exist in Chinese and Japanese).
3. The phonetic sequence of the target language is mapped into characters in the target language (e.g., Chinese characters).

The above processes are similar when used on different languages. Here, we use English-Chinese transliteration as an example to illustrate the general process. Figure 3.7 shows an example of transliteration between an English name (Frances Taylor) and its transliteration in Chinese (弗朗西丝泰勒):

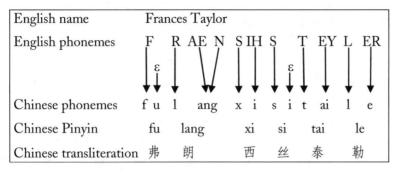

English name	Frances Taylor										
English phonemes	F	R AE N	S IH S		T EY L ER						
Chinese phonemes	f u	l	ang	x	i	s	i	t	ai	l	e
Chinese Pinyin	fu	lang		xi		si		tai		le	
Chinese transliteration	弗	朗		西		丝		泰		勒	

FIGURE 3.7: Illustration of transliteration from English to Chinese (from Cao et al., 2007b),

The transliteration process bears much in common with SMT. Let us assume that the English name corresponds to a sequence of phones $E = e_1 e_2 \ldots e_m$, and the Chinese name to $C = c_1 c_2 \ldots c_n$, where c_i and e_j represent respectively a Chinese and English phonetic unit. The probability to translate the English name to Chinese name is expressed as $P(C|E)$. We can follow the approach of statistical MT (Brown et al., 1993) by assuming an alignment $A = a_1 a_2 \ldots a_n$ between the two strings, where a_i denotes the position of English phonetic unit corresponding to the i-th Chinese phonetic unit. As in word alignment in SMT, an empty unit ε is inserted in the source language. Different from word alignment, here the phonetic alignments are not allowed to cross. As in phrase-based SMT, a sequence of consecutive phonetic units can be grouped together. Let us denote the phonetic "phrases" by C_i and E_i. Then the transliteration probability can be expressed as follows:

$$P(C|E) = \sum_A P(C, A|E) = \sum_A \prod_i P(C_i | E_i) P(n_i | m_i)$$

where n_i and m_i are the lengths of Chinese and English phonetic "phrases." $P(C_i | E_i)$ represents the transliteration probability between the two sub-sequences, and $P(n_i | m_i)$ the length-based alignment probability. Using the maximum approximation, we have:

$$P(C|E) \approx P(C, A^*|E)$$

where

$$A^* = \arg\max_A P(C, A|E) = \arg\max_A \prod_i P(C_i | E_i) P(n_i | m_i)$$

As in sentence alignment, we can consider several types of alignment between phonetic sequences: 1-1, 1-2, 2-1, 0-1, 1-0, and 2-2. Then given a set of training transliteration examples, the EM algorithm can be used to train both $P(C_i \mid E_i)$ and $P(n_i \mid m_i)$.

The conversion of Chinese to Pinyin sequence can be performed by a lookup in the conversion table. Many Chinese dictionaries contain the pronunciation in Pinyin. Although there can be some ambiguities, i.e., a Chinese character can be pronounced in different ways (e.g., 解 as *Xie* when it is used as a family name, or *Jie* otherwise), these cases are relatively infrequent in transliteration. In particular, when a foreign name is translated into Chinese, only a limited number of Chinese characters are used.

For English pronunciation, one can also use a conversion table. An example of such a table is the CMU pronunciation dictionary,[5] which stores 125,000 English words (including a number of proper names) and their phonetic transcriptions. Rules can also be used to convert English character strings to syllable sequences (Wan and Verspoor, 1998). This latter approach is more capable of dealing with OOV. The specific process is beyond the scope of this book. We will not describe more details about it here.

The above description provides one way to perform transliteration. Notice that there are several variants, in particular, in the way that transliteration probability is determined. Interested readers can refer to the following references: Cao et al. (2007b) Chen et al. (2006) for English–Chinese, Kang and Choi (2000) for English–Korean, Qu et al. (2003) for English–Japanese, and AbdulJaleel and Larkey (2003) for English–Arabic.

All the studies on CLIR using transliteration have proven that transliteration is very useful to complement the other translation methods in query translation.

3.7.3 Mining Translations Using Hyperlinks

General translation and transliteration can solve a major part of the translation problems in CLIR. However, there are still exceptions that cannot be dealt with correctly by them. Some proper names of persons and companies may fall into this category. For example, the company name "Sony" is transliterated in to "索尼" (pronounced as *So Ni* in Pinyin) in simplified Chinese, but it is translated as "新力" (pronounced as *Xin Li*) in traditional Chinese in Taiwan, Hong Kong, Macau, and South Asia Chinese communities till 2009. Similarly, "General Electric" or "GE" is translated literally into simplified Chinese as "通用电气," but phonetically into traditional Chinese as "奇异" (pronunciation similar to the letters G and E). These translations cannot be found using general translation tools or transliteration.

To solve this problem, Lu et al. (2004) exploited hyperlinks on the Web to determine possible name equivalence in different languages. They observed that anchor texts in different language

---

[5] http://www.speech.cs.cmu.edu/cgi-bin/cmudict

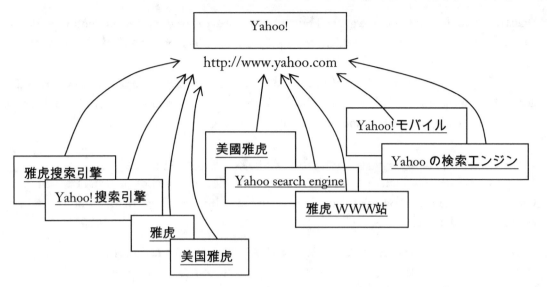

FIGURE 3.8: Illustration of hyperlinks and anchor texts to the Web page www.yahoo.com (adapted from Lu et al., 2004).

referring to the same web page are often name variants in different languages. For example, the website "www.yahoo.com" can often be referred to with anchor texts such as: "雅虎搜索引擎," "美国雅虎," "yahoo!," "Yahoo!モバイル," "Yahooの検索エンジン," etc. (see Figure 3.8).

Therefore, they considered the anchor texts referring to the same Web page to be parallel or comparable, and try to extract equivalent names from them. Assuming a set of URLs $U=\{u_1, ..., u_n\}$ linking to the same Web page with their respective anchor texts, the correspondence between two terms s and t in anchor texts of two different languages is estimated as follows:

$$P(s \leftrightarrow t) = \frac{P(s \cap t)}{P(s \cup t)} = \frac{\sum_{i=1}^{n} P(s \cap t \mid u_i) P(u_i)}{\sum_{i=1}^{n} P(s \cup t \mid u_i) P(u_i)}$$

$$\approx \frac{\sum_{i=1}^{n} P(s \mid u_i) P(t \mid u_i) P(u_i)}{\sum_{i=1}^{n} [P(s \mid u_i) + P(t \mid u_i) - P(s \mid u_i) P(t \mid u_i)] P(u_i)}$$

The last step assumes that s and t are independent given u_i. This mining process enabled them to find translations for new terms, or new translations. For example, the following correct translations are found for "National Palace Museum": 故宫, 故宫博物院, 国立故宫博物院, while these translations are not stored in the general bilingual dictionary they used. The method is particularly useful for extracting particular translations of proper names such as "新力," "索尼," and "ソニー" for "Sony."

The mined translations have been used in a CLIR experiment. The result showed that these additional translations can help improve CLIR effectiveness. This mining process is a good complement to the existing translation and transliteration methods.

3.7.4 Mining Translations from Monolingual Web Pages

Many translations/transliterations may have been embedded in monolingual texts. For example, in Chinese texts, the name "Barack Obama" can be followed by its Chinese translation(s) as shown in the following example:

> 现在网上最热的词条，就是这个"Barack Obama," 巴拉
> 克·欧巴马（巴拉克·奥巴马）。 为什么？2007年2月10
> 日，他正式宣布参选2008年美国总统。...

In this example, two transliterations of "Barack Obama" are provided after it: "巴拉克·欧巴马" and "巴拉克·奥巴马." If one thinks that these translitarations can be determined automatically using the transliteration approach described earlier, the following example from a page on Wikipedia shows a case that cannot be dealt with by transliteration—"Steven Chu" is not a transliteration of the Chinese name "朱棣文":

朱棣文（Steven Chu，1948年2月28日－），美国华裔物理学家，生于美国圣路易斯；

Similar examples are "张任谦" (Chang Yam Him, Victor Chang) and "姚期智" (Andrew Yao).

New technical terms also may not have their recognized translations. These terms are also often used in monolingual texts with their translations, for example:

这就诞生了潜语义索引(Latent Semantic Indexing) . . .

The co-occurrence of a proper name or a technical term with its translation is a widely spread phenomenon in monolingual texts. Zhang and Vines (2004) further observed that such co-occurrences usually follow some patterns. For example, the original name is often followed by its translation/transliteration, and the latter is put in parentheses (e.g., "Barack Obama (巴拉克·欧巴马)") or separated with comma (e.g., "Barack Obama, 巴拉克·欧巴马"). To retrieve such translations, they take advantage of a search engine to retrieve possible instances corresponding to the patterns. For example, one can issue a query using the terms in one language (e.g., "Barack Obama") and specify to find documents in Chinese. The passage we illustrated earlier could be retrieved. Instances corresponding to the patterns are extracted from the top returned documents (or snippets) and a statistical analysis follows in order to keep the strong translations. This allows them to find translations for specific terms and proper names that are not stored in the dictionary.

The approach of Zhang and Vine are followed in several other studies (Cheng et al., 2004; Huang et al., 2005; Kuo et al., 2006). Some other studies try to refine the extraction process. For example, a problem that Zhang et al. (2005) and Huang et al. (2005) observed is that wrong instances can be identified using the patterns used by Zhang and Vines (2004). To reduce such noise instances, they propose to add strongly related terms in the query issued to a search engine. For example, to identify the English translation of 列夫.托尔斯泰 (Leo Tolstoy), they add the translation of the related terms to it such as "war," "peace" for "战争与和平," called *hint words*, to enhance the search queries as follows: "列夫.托尔斯泰+war" and "列夫.托尔斯泰+peace." The addition of hint words allows them to retrieve a set of less noisy snippets. Li et al. (2009) used a similar approach to find OOV translations between Korean–English and Chinese–English.

What we notice in the above approaches is that the translations are determined on the fly when the translations of some terms are required. Although the approach is flexible, it may require some extra time for the online processing. Nevertheless, the approach is not limited to an online processing and can well be used in offline mode to extract a dictionary. This is performed in Cao et al. (2007b) on a large Web collection. In Cao et al. (2007b) the possible translation candidates are also identified using a set of predefined patterns, similar to Zhang and Vines (2004). Below are some examples of the extracted instances (where the underlined parts are the correct translations to be identified):

> 我的朋友维尔克 (Velker)
> 就到了财政花园(TREASURY GARDENS)
> 而包括通用电气塑料(GE Plastics)
> 又称特征检测(Signature-based detection)
> 入侵检测系统的特征检测(Signature-based detection)
> 维多利亚大学(University of Victoria)

The problem now is to extract the correct translation candidate in each instance. One simple method is to serve the frequency of the extracted instances to determine the most frequent candidate. For instance, from the above extracted instances, one can observe that the string 特征检测 appears multiple times before the term "Signature-based detection." It thus has a higher chance to be considered as the translation of the latter term, than another string, say 系统的特征检测. However, this does not solve all the problems. For example, the correct translation 特征检测 preceded by a functional character 的 (of) can also have quite a high frequency. So is a shorter term 检测. Two possible solutions can be used:

1. one can use some heuristic rules to filter out these cases;
2. one can also use a method similar to SMT that tries to align the term and its possible candidates.

Cao et al. use the second approach. It works as follows. Given the following extracted instance for "Signature-based detection":

... 入侵检测系统的特征检测 (Signature-based detection).

We assume that all the following strings are possible candidate translations for it:

检测

特征检测

系统的特征检测

检测系统的特征检测

入侵检测系统的特征检测

The problem is equivalent to determine the boundary (in this case, to the left) of the correct translation. This problem can be cast as an alignment problem: we try to align the English term in the parentheses to possible Chinese segments through both translation and transliteration. The best-aligned segment is considered to be the translation. For the first example, the translation in the instance "我的朋友维尔克 (Velker)" can be obtained by transliteration. The translation in "入侵检测系统的特征检测 (Signature-based detection)" can be determined through translation (特征-signature and 检测-detection); while the instance "维多利亚大学(University of Victoria)" requires the use of both translation (for "University") and transliteration (for "Victoria"). In the approach of (Cao et al. 2007b), a binary classifier is used to separate translation from transliteration in the candidate string. However, other methods could be used within an integrated alignment process in which both transliteration and translation probabilities are considered.

The translations mined from a corpus by the above methods have been used to complement an existing bilingual dictionary. In general, the mined dictionary contributes in increasing the coverage of the existing dictionary, both in terms of source-language terms and the target-language translations. In the experiments of Cao et al. on TREC-5&6 and TREC-9 English–Chinese collections, the mined translation relations have led to significant improvements in retrieval effectiveness, compared to the utilization of the bilingual dictionary (LDC dictionary) alone: the MAP is increased from 0.2839 (for TREC-5&6) and 0.2020 (for TREC-9) with the LDC dictionary to 0.2963 and 0.2367 using both LDC and the mined dictionary. In particular, several unknown words by the LDC dictionary can be correctly translated by the generated bilingual lexicon. In Li et al. (2009) the CLIR experiments on the NTCIR-3 English collection also showed that when the extracted OOV translations are used to enhance a dictionary, the retrieval effectiveness can be largely increased: from 0.212 to 0.256 in relaxed MAP and from 0.223 to 0.265 in rigid MAP.

Instead of mining translations from a general web corpus, one can also use a more specific corpus. Wikipedia is such a resource often exploited. In addition to the above approaches, Wikipedia also offers the possibility to exploit the hyperlinks created between articles in multiple languages. Jones et al. (2008) exploited this property to identify the corresponding articles in different languages, and they assumed the basenames of these articles (the name listed in Wikipedia hierarchy for the article) to be mutual translations. However, this simple approach does not perform a deep mining in Wikipedia and only a limited number of translation relations can be extracted between basenames. A more thorough exploitation could rely on methods used on comparable texts: the multiple versions are indeed comparable texts. Such an approach is used in Schönhofen et al. (2007). The corresponding Wikipedia texts in Hungarian and English are exploited using pseudo-relevance feedback mechanism so as to identify additional related terms in another language. The experiments showed that the mined relations can significantly increase the retrieval effectiveness over a method using a dictionary (SZTAKI Szótár) alone.

All the experiments we described above confirm that the Web is a rich resource for translation relations, and one can extract appropriate translations from it for various types of element, in particular, for OOV translation. The approaches proposed till now are far from exhaustive. New methods could be developed to mine (loose) translation relations for CLIR purposes.

·   ·   ·   ·

CHAPTER 4

Other Methods to Improve CLIR

The previous chapters described the main approaches for query translation. In this chapter, we describe several specific techniques to further improve CLIR.

4.1 PRE- AND POST-TRANSLATION EXPANSION

As we stated earlier, one of the main differences between query translation and full text MT is that query translation is not limited to one translation per word, neither to literal translations. Translations for a query can be terms related to it. For example, even if the French word "hôpital" is not a translation of a query on "health care," adding the term into the French translation of this query may be beneficial. The question is how to select those target language words that are strongly related to the query in the source language.

The idea exploited in pre- and post-translation expansion is similar to pseudo-relevance feedback. Pre-translation expansion uses the original query to retrieve a set of documents from a collection in the source language. A set of terms are extracted from them and added into the query before translation.

Post-translation expansion is more similar to traditional pseudo-relevance feedback: a set of target-language documents are retrieved using the translated query, and a set of terms are extracted from them and used to enhance the query. A new retrieval is finally performed to retrieve a new set of documents.

Several studies have tested both pre- and post-translation expansions. Ballesteros and Croft (1997) found that both pre- and post-translation expansions can improve both precision and recall. McNamee and Mayfield (2002) showed that pre-translation is more useful than post-translation, while Levow et al. (2005) found the reverse.

Overall, both expansion processes have shown to be able to improve the retrieval effectiveness to some degree, but there is no clear conclusion that one expansion is better than another. The impact of these expansion processes strong depends on the document collections from which the expansion terms are extracted. While it is the case that post-translation expansion is generally based on a set of target-language documents retrieved from the same collection as the collection on which the final search is performed, one has to use a different document collection for pre-translation expansion. The difference between this collection and the one on which search is performed can explain the large differences observed on the impact of pre-translation expansion: when these collections cover similar topics, one could expect that pre-translation expansion can find additional terms strongly related to the query before the translation. If, on the contrary, the collections cover very different topics, then pre-translation expansion could be even harmful. For example, if the query "drug traffic" is expanded before translation using a medical document collection in English, and then searched on a general French collection, one would expect a drift of the query toward the "legal medication" sense, which is harmful. So the collection used for pre-translation expansion should be strongly related to the query topics.

4.2   FUZZY MATCHING

Terms in similar languages (languages within the same linguistic family) can be similar and only change slightly from a language to another. This is the case between Scandinavian languages (Swedish, Finish) and between several other European language (Spanish, English, and French). CLIR between similar languages can be performed even without a true translation by applying fuzzy matching. Among the first CLIR experiments on French documents in TREC, Buckley et al. (2000) exploited the similarity between French and English, and treated a French query as a "misspelled" English sentence. They used a simple French stemmer to stem French words, which are then matched directly against English documents (stemmed by an English stemmer) without translation. This is indeed a utilization of French–English cognates. Their experiments showed that without any specific translation, this fuzzy matching process can successfully retrieve documents in another language at a remarkable level of effectiveness: about 50% of that of monolingual retrieval, which is equivalent to the simple method based on dictionaries. This experiment shows the potential of using a fuzzy matching for CLIR between similar languages.

Following a similar idea, McNamee and Mayfield (2002, 2004b) used character n-grams to perform CLIR between European languages. Between similar languages, character n-grams can allow matching similar terms. For example, "information" in English, French, and German share several n-grams (e.g., 4-grams) with the Spanish word "información" and Italian word "informazione." This will enable them to match each other to some extent.

However, the flexibility of fuzzy matching is not only an advantage. It is also a source of problems. Words that are similar (e.g., they share some n-grams) in two languages may not be related. This is the case for "chair" in English and "chaire" in French. One can find many other examples. There is thus a high risk to match a term with unrelated terms in other languages.

The effectiveness using fuzzy matching or n-gram matching is usually lower than approaches using reasonable translation resources and tools. Therefore, the n-gram-based matching is to be used only when no better resource is available, or as a complementary tool to other translation resources and tools.

Instead of comparing *n*-grams, Pirkola et al. (2003) used more sophisticated approaches to determine possible matching terms between two languages:

1.   terms in two languages that have small edit distance are considered to match;
2.   if a term can be transformed to a term in another language using some morphological rules, then the second term is considered to match the former.

The second approach has been tested on several languages (French, Spanish, Finish, German, and English). For example, the Finish word *konvektio* can be transformed into its equivalent in English *convection* by applying the following transformation rules: *o→on* (at the end of a word), *ko→co* (at the beginning), and *ekt→ect* (in the middle). The key problem is to determine the correct transformation rules to apply. To this end, Pirkola et al. (2003) have tried to automatically extract transformation rules from a bilingual dictionary: if a bigram or trigram within a word often corresponds to a unigram/bigram/trigram in the target language word, then the transformation is possibly a valid one between these languages. Pirkola showed that the transformation rules extracted can identify more or less correct translation candidates, depending on the topic area. For example, in the biology area, the transformation rules combined with edit distance can successfully find the correct English translation word for Spanish words among the top 4 candidates in 80% of the cases. When the transformation rules are used on top of a dictionary to help select the most appropriate translation candidates, the CLIR effectiveness can be improved significantly, compared to the approach that uses only the bilingual dictionary (Pirkola et al., 2007).

This series of experiments show that the similarity between languages can help CLIR, and this similarity should be fully exploited.

4.3   COMBINING TRANSLATIONS

Translation resources have often been combined in order to produce better translations. For example, Lu et al. (2004) combined statistical a translation model with a bilingual dictionary. Their experiments on NTCIR-2 English–Chinese collection showed that the approach was able to increase the CLIR effectiveness (MAP) from 0.155 with the statistical model alone and 0.143 with the dictionary alone to 0.235 with both. Several other studies have also combined different translation resources for different languages (Shi et al., 2007; Chen et al., 2000; Jones et al., 2007), which all showed improvements in CLIR effectiveness. The general approach can be described as follows: Each translation resource is used to suggest a list of translation candidates, and the different lists are combined to produce the final list of translations.

Translations in both directions, i.e., from the source language to the target language and the reverse, can also be combined. This combination can help deal with the problem of translation ambiguities. The assumption made here is that translations of a given word can be more specific or more generic, especially when a statistical translation model is used. In this case, more specific translations are preferred because more general translations can be more ambiguous. To distinguish specific translation terms from more generic ones, a possible heuristic is as follows: a more specific translation candidate could likely be retranslated back to the same source term with a relatively high probability, while a more generic or ambiguous translation term would likely also generate many other translations in the source language, leading to a low backward translation probability to the same source term. For example, when we use a statistical translation model, frequent French terms such as "prendre" (take), "pouvoir" (can) have often been suggested as strong translation candidates for many queries in the source language (English). However, these general words in French, when retranslated back to English, would generate many English words as translations, all with relatively small probabilities. So, the backward translation probability of these words to the given query term will be very low. This provides a possible solution to select more specific translations by combining the translations between terms in both directions. For example, one can define a new weight as the arithmetic average or geometric average of the translation probabilities in both directions:

$$w(s,t) = [P(t|s) + P(s|t)]/2, \text{ or}$$

$$w(s,t) = [P(t|s)\, P(s|t)]^{1/2}$$

The above approach has been used in Nie and Simard (2001) and Wang and Oard (2006). In Nie and Simard (2001), no improvement has been obtained using this approach, compared to a translation in one direction only. A possible reason is that the idf factor has been combined with the translation probability, and this factor can naturally decrease the importance of frequent terms in the target language even if their translation probability is strong. So the addition of reverse translation probability did not show to be much useful.

The investigations on bidirectional translation are not limited to the term level. One can also perform a bidirectional translation using both query and document translations. Each of the approaches will result in a ranking list, and the two lists can be combined to produce a final list. McCarley (1999) tested such a combination approach on TREC 6 and 7 French–English collections. The results showed that this approach can outperform the unidirectional translation approach, which uses either document translation or query translation alone. This experiment suggests the potential benefit of using both query and document translations. However, one also has to notice the additional cost associated to this.

4.4   TRANSITIVE TRANSLATION

Although there are many resources for translation between English and many languages, there may be much less for translation between other language pairs, for example, between Chinese and

French, Japanese and Swedish, and so on. It is then interesting to see if one can use a third language such as English as a pivot language to perform CLIR between these languages. Such an approach is called *transitive translation*.

Several studies have been carried out to test the effectiveness of such an approach. Kishida and Kando (2005) examined the German–French translation via English as pivot language. Similarly, Gey et al. (1999), Hiemstra and Kraaij (1998), Lin and Chen (2003), and Chen and Gey (2003) have also examined the utilization of a pivot language (English) to perform transitive translation between French–German, German–Italian, and Japanese–Chinese. All the above studies made the same observation: while no direct translation is possible, transitive translation could help identify some useful documents. Not surprisingly, transitive translation usually performs worse than direct translation (although there are some exceptions Lehtokangas et al., 2004).

In TREC-7, Franz et al. (1999) have compared the following approaches for transitive CLIR between English and German using document translation:

- Transitive translation of documents: German documents are translated into French, which is then translated into English.
- Convolution translation model: Statistical translation models of German to French and French to English are combined as follows (where f, g and e represent, respectively, a French, German and English word):

$$t(g \mid e) = \sum_f t(g \mid f) t(f \mid e)$$

This new translation model is used to translate German documents to English.

Franz et al. noted a large difference between the above two approaches: The first approach achieved an effectiveness of 45% of the monolingual effectiveness, while the convolution translation model only achieved 37%. This comparison suggests the following interesting observation: while for query translation it is often desirable to include multiple translations for each term to produce a query expansion effect, this is not necessarily desirable for document translation, especially when transitional translation is used. In fact, at each translation step in the above convolution translation model, multiple translations will be suggested and these suggestions will simply be handed over to the next translation step without making any selection. The final translation model will likely to be very noisy. In comparison, the transitive translation of documents made a selection of the best translation term at each step, allowing prune off a large amount of noise for the next translation step. This pruning can be considered as an implicit utilization of document context to select the best translation candidates. This fact may explain the difference in retrieval effectiveness between the two approaches.

In Gollins and Sanderson (2001), transitive CLIR is performed through *triangulation*, i.e., to combine several transitive translations through several pivot languages. However, their experimental experiments did not show that the approach can produce a result comparable to a direct translation. This is not surprising. Similar idea is exploited later by Lehtokangas et al. (2004); but in addition, Lehtokangas et al. also used structured query translation (e.g. to combine synonyms) to cope with the problem of translation disambiguation. Each translation path also exploits better resources and methods (dictionary, fuzzy matching, and so on). These additional means have helped them to produce competitive result to direct translation: Their results on CLEF 2001 and 2002 data showed that transitive CLIR can arrive at the same level of effectiveness as a direct translation approach. This result is interesting: it shows the potential of using one or several pivot languages to perform transitive CLIR when a direct translation is impossible.

4.5 INTEGRATING MONOLINGUAL AND TRANSLINGUAL RELATIONS

Several studies we have described suggest that the relationships between terms in the same language can be useful to CLIR. For example, the approaches of (Gao et al. 2001) and (Liu et al. 2005) used monolingual cohesion to select translation terms in the target language. The approaches of pre- and post-translation expansion try to identify related terms in the same language(s). All these approaches have proven to be useful. However, monolingual and translingual relations have been considered separately in these studies. A natural question is: can we consider them within a unified framework? Would this be useful?

Cao et al. (2007a) recently tested such an integrated approach, and have found it very useful. In Cao et al. (2007a), both translingual and monolingual relations between terms in two languages are represented in the same graph (as shown in Figure 4.1). Two types of monolingual relations are considered in this study: *contain* and *co-occur*. The former is used to link a phrase to its constituent words. This relation is particularly important in East-Asian languages, where a sentence can be segmented into longer or shorter words. For example, 程序设计 (program design, programming) can be considered as a single word (or phrase) or as two words 程序 (program) and 设计 (design). In this case, we consider that 程序设计 *contains* 程序 and 设计. The second relation links terms that co-occur frequently in documents. This type of relation has proven particularly useful in monolingual IR. Translingual relations are those stored in a bilingual dictionary. Let us assume an English–Chinese dictionary containing the following entries (in which we add the English translations between parentheses):

> article: 冠词 (determinant), 论文 (paper), 物品 (object)
> program design: 程序设计
> program: 程序 ([computer] program), 节目 ([TV] program).

Given a query "articles about program design," the following (segment of) graph could be created, in which nodes represent terms in both languages, links represent relations:

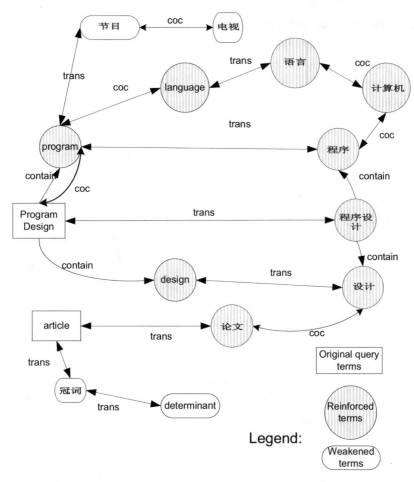

FIGURE 4.1: An illustration of a graph integrating both monolingual and translingual relationships (Cao et al., 2007a).

We can see that the original query terms are linked to other English and Chinese terms through different paths. Intuitively, the more there are paths between two nodes, the stronger the relation is. The question for query translation is to select the appropriate translation terms (in Chinese) for the context of the query. In order to do this, Cao et al. use the intuition that the correct translation terms are more mutually connected in the graph and can reinforce each other, while incorrect translation terms are merely connected to other nodes and they cannot be reinforced. Therefore, they propose to implement the selection of translation terms as random walks in the graph from the nodes corresponding to the original query terms. The probability attributed to each node at the end of the process will indicate how appropriate the corresponding translation term could be for the query. Notice also that this approach naturally provides some capability for translation disambiguation.

As we can see in the figure, the relevant translations for the ambiguous query words "program" and "article" are more connected. The selection or enhancement of these translations is indeed due to the context of words in the query. Such a context-dependent selection and weighting of translation terms is crucial in query translation.

More specifically, the transition from any node n_i to node n_j is estimated as follows:

$$M_{ij} = \begin{cases} (1-\gamma)\sum_{l \in L} P(n_j \mid l, n_i)P(l) & n_i \neq n_j \\ \gamma & n_i = n_j \end{cases}$$

where l is a type of link (translate, co-occur or contain), and $0 < \gamma < 1$ is a constant corresponding to the probability of staying at the same node. $P(l)$ is the prior of following a link of the type l, which can be determined using a set of training queries. After k steps of random walk, we have the following transition matrix:

$$M_{ij}^{(k)} = (\gamma \sum_{t=0}^{k} (1-\gamma)M^t)_{ij}$$

The transition from the query Q to every term can be expressed as follows:

$$\theta_Q^{(k)} = \theta_Q^0 M^{(k)}$$

where θ_Q^0 is the initial query model and $\theta_Q^{(k)}$ the final query model, which attributes probabilities to terms in both languages. What will be used is the set of Chinese terms. Documents can be ranked according to the following score:

$$\text{score}(Q, D) = \sum_{t \in V} P(t \mid \theta_Q^{(k)}) \log P(t \mid \theta_D)$$

in which V is the vocabulary in the target language. The experiments reported in Cao et al. (2007a) showed that this model can significantly outperform the previous translation approaches using only the translation relation. On two TREC collections for English–Chinese CLIR, the effectiveness obtained is equivalent to that of the monolingual IR, which is higher than the usual figure of 60–80% for the collections.

The integrated approach also outperforms the pre- and post-translation expansion approaches. Indeed, a form of pre- and post-translation expansion is naturally integrated in the above approach. This leads to an interesting observation: In the integrated approach, several types of term relationship can be combined in random walks in more appropriate way, while in separate pre- and post-translation expansions, parameters have to be set manually and separately, not always at the optimal level. This study shows a promising direction for future development of CLIR: the integration of translation and expansion in the same process and model. To our knowledge, this is the only study in this direction. Further investigation is required to exploit the full potential of such an approach.

4.6   DISCUSSIONS

In this chapter, we described several approaches trying to further improve the effectiveness of CLIR. The approaches described point to the following directions:

- Exploiting more translation resources: one can extend the translation by using different translation relations—fuzzy matching, bidirectional translation, and by combining multiple translation resources.
- Combining monolingual and translingual relations: monolingual relations can help query translation. It is possible to integrate those relations together with translation relations within a unified framework of query translation.
- Finally, context clearly proves itself as an important factor to be considered during translation.

The investigations on the above aspects are only at their beginning. Much work still remains to be done. For example, while structured translation has been proposed by Pirkola et al., query structure is generally not recognized and used during translation. Query terms are considered to be independent during translation, or at the best, forming a flat structure. In many cases, it is crucial to recognize the inherent structure or dependency among the terms in the query to determine the correct translations. For example, given a query "computer architecture design," if we fail to recognize the strong dependency between "computer" and "architecture," the query could be translated in the meaning of "architecture design," which is "建筑设计" in Chinese, while the correct translation should be "计算机体系结构设计." This problem is crucial not only in CLIR, but also in general IR. Approaches have been proposed to consider the query structure or term dependencies in monolingual IR, such as Gao et al. (2004a) and Metzler and Croft (2005). In future CLIR studies, one could inspire from the studies in monolingual IR.

Finally, query translation can be performed in interaction with the user. Several studies on interactive CLIR have been carried out (Sheridan and Ballerini, 1996; Oard et al., 2008; Oard et al., 2004; López-Ostenero et al., 2005), which proposed to provide the user with a rough backward translation of the translated query (nouns or noun phrases in it) by using a bilingual glossary or dictionary, or to provide a cross-language summary of the returned documents. Based on that the user can choose the appropriate terms in the target language. Interactive CLIR is helpful for a class of users who have some knowledge of the target language or who are willing to perform precise search. However, the experiments are difficult to compare to the other approaches we described in this book, which are fully automatic. We will not describe these approaches in more detail here.

CHAPTER 5

A Look into the Future: Toward a Unified View of Monolingual IR and CLIR?

5.1 WHAT HAS BEEN ACHIEVED?

So far in this book, we have described the problems that have arisen in CLIR, namely, the translation problems. We have treated them as the problems on top of monolingual IR. The translation problems have been dealt with using the following means:

- Using an off-the-shelve MT system;
- Using a bilingual dictionary or thesaurus;
- Using parallel or comparable corpora.

In this book, we have described these approaches and discussed about their suitability to CLIR. In addition to these main approaches, we also described various complementary methods proposed in the area, such as pre- and post-translation query expansion, fuzzy matching, and so on.

All the above approaches have led to some success in TREC-like experiments. In general, for resource-rich language pairs, we can usually achieve retrieval effectiveness at the level of 80–100% of that of monolingual IR. In some of the experiments, CLIR effectiveness is even higher than monolingual IR effectiveness. We could say that CLIR for these languages can be performed without much loss in effectiveness, compared to monolingual IR. This observation tends to suggest that CLIR technology becomes mature to be used by end users.

However, we have to keep in mind that we only dealt with one of the problems in CLIR: retrieving relevant documents in another language. Another important problem is to make the retrieved documents understandable to the user, which is not always a trivial task. Indeed, the second problem represents a more serious obstacle to the practical uses of CLIR than the cross-language retrieval problem we described. For many languages, we still do not have decent MT systems available. Fortunately, MT systems have been much improved during the last decade. For resource-rich language pairs, the translations are usually understandable by human readers. So, one can foresee a combination of CLIR method and MT translation of the retrieved documents as the most suitable solution for end users. Indeed, such a solution is offered by current search engines such as Google, however, with a direct query translation by MT.

On the techniques for CLIR, despite the encouraging results obtained so far, there is still room for further improvements. Even if CLIR achieves an effectiveness level of 90% of the monolingual IR, the difference is still quite large, given the fact that the current IR systems and search engines often try to improve retrieval effectiveness by very small percentages (e.g., 1–2%). There may be two places where further improvements can be made:

1.   Translation resources and tools can always be improved. As we showed in this book, a better translation usually result in a better CLIR result. So, continuous efforts should be made to further improve the translation quality. However, as we have also made it clear, the improvement of translation in CLIR is different from that in MT. So, an area of research on CLIR is to develop specific methods for translation in CLIR.

2.   The CLIR problems are currently perceived as an addition of translation on top of a monolingual IR. This view can be expressed by the following equation:

$$CLIR = translation + monolingual\ IR.$$

The translation problem has often been dealt with from a pure translation point of view. Despite some adaptations, the main principle is the same as in general MT. For example, statistical translation models used in CLIR are usually the same as those in MT, whose goal is to maximize a quality measure for general translation. We argue here that the translation problem is an integral part of the whole CLIR problem, and unified CLIR models integrating translation should be defined. We believe that this is another area where further improvements can be brought to CLIR.

In the following section, we will show that the fundamental problems of CLIR and monolingual IR are indeed quite similar (despite the language difference). This comparison will suggest that the approaches proposed for query expansion and analysis in monolingual IR could be adapted to query translation in CLIR.

5.2   INSPIRING FROM MONOLINGUAL IR

5.2.1   Parallel Between Query Expansion and Query Translation

As we described in Section 1.2.2, query expansion is a common approach to improve IR effectiveness. The basic idea is to enhance the original query by adding some related terms in it. The key to the success of query expansion is (1) determining terms that are strongly related to the query; (2) properly weighting the expansion terms with respect to the original terms. We described three commons methods to identify expansion terms:

- Using a thesaurus: related terms are identified from a thesaurus such as Wordnet (Voorhees, 1994).
- Using co-occurrence analysis: frequently co-occurring terms in the documents are used to enhance the initial query.
- Using pseudo-relevance feedback documents: the terms extracted from the top-ranked documents are assumed to be related to the query.

Comparing these approaches to the approaches to CLIR we described in this book, one can immediately notice a strong similarity between them:

- Dictionary-based translation vs. thesaurus-based expansion: a bilingual dictionary or a multilingual thesaurus plays a similar role in CLIR to a monolingual thesaurus in monolingual IR. In both cases, we rely on the relations stored in manually constructed lexical resources to determine related terms in the same language or in a different language (i.e., translations).
- Translation based on parallel and comparable corpora vs. co-occurrence analysis: the extraction of cross-language similarity relations between terms in two languages from a parallel corpus or a comparable corpus (Braschler and Schäuble, 2001) can be viewed as an approach similar to co-occurrence analysis in monolingual IR. The co-occurrence analysis used in monolingual IR has been indeed extended to comparable and parallel texts. The only difference lies in the fact that co-occurrences in the latter case are in the corresponding texts in two languages. Statistical translation models (IBM models) can also be viewed as a more sophisticated cross-language co-occurrence analysis using aligned sentences. Different from the static analysis used in cross-language term similarity, the training of a statistical model uses a dynamic process to determine relations so as to maximize the correspondence between the given parallel sentences. This is more a difference of implementation than that of principle. To further show the similarity, let us imagine a parallel corpus in which a text is aligned to itself. Then a statistical translation model trained on such a parallel corpus will encode monolingual term similarity. This is indeed very similar to co-occurrence analysis: terms that co-occur in the same text will be considered to be similar. This idea has been successfully exploited for monolingual IR in Berger and Lafferty (1999), in which the resulting monolingual term similarity (or translation) is used in document expansion. We can

see here that despite the language difference between translation model and monolingual co-occurrence analysis, both are based on the same principle.

- Pseudo-relevance feedback vs. post-translation expansion: Post-translation expansion is a cross-language pseudo-relevance feedback process, i.e., to identify pseudo-feedback documents in another language. The relationship is obvious.

The above comparison draws a clear picture that many approaches to CLIR have their counterparts in monolingual IR. Namely, most query translation approaches can be cast as a special case of query expansion in monolingual IR, with the difference that the "expansion" is made by terms in a different language and that the original terms are no longer used after "expansion." This suggests that the methods developed for query expansion in monolingual IR can usually be adapted to query translation in CLIR.

Notice that the above statement does not mean that the language difference between query expansion in monolingual IR and query translation in CLIR is not important. On the contrary, as we have seen in this book, most approaches for CLIR specifically target the problems arisen from the language differences. What is stated is that, despite the languages differences, the two problems share many common issues, and similar approaches (or principles) can be used to deal with both of them.

Let us now put the two processes into a common framework. In fact, in both cases, our goal is to determine the terms that are semantically *implied* by the original query. By implication, we mean that a term (or rather the meaning of a term) is entailed by the original query expression (or what is meant by it). Let us represent it by the symbol $\rightarrow$: $Q \rightarrow t$ means that the term t is implied by Q. For example, given a query Q: "prevention of H1N1 spreading" in English, one can identify (using different resources) that the following English terms represent meanings that are implied by the query: virus, swine flu, virus transmission, pandemic, vaccine, vaccination campaign, and so on. This can be expressed as the following implication relations:

$$Q \rightarrow \text{virus}$$
$$Q \rightarrow \text{swine flu}$$
$$Q \rightarrow \text{virus transmission}$$
$$Q \rightarrow \text{vaccine}$$
$$\dots$$

In the CLIR context, we can also identify the following translation terms in other languages that mean the same thing: prévention, H1N1, transmission (in French) and 预防, H1N1, 传播 (in Chinese). These translation terms can also be expressed by implication relations as follows:

$$Q \rightarrow \text{prévention}$$
$$Q \rightarrow \text{H1N1}$$

$$Q \to \text{transmission}$$
$$Q \to 预防$$
$$Q \to 传播$$

If our goal is to just identify those translation terms that mean the same thing as the original query terms, we are indeed doing a strict translation. Still, such a translation can be seen as trying to identify the strictly implied terms in a different language.

More generally, we also try to identify less strictly implied terms such as: pandémie, grippe porcine, campagne de vaccination, contamination, etc. (in French) and 大流行, 瘟疫, 猪流感, 疫苗, 传染, etc. (in Chinese). These terms are strongly related to the query without being its translations. The implication relation can also be extended between Q and these terms.

So, given a query Q, the key problem in both query expansion in monolingual IR and query translation in CLIR is to determine the terms which are implied by Q. This is the first problem we described for query expansion in Section 1.2.2.

The second problem is term weighting, which is related to how strong the implication relation is. This aspect is not expressed in the above examples. However, for query expansion, one can express the weight of an expansion term as as a measure of the degree of implication. A more general expression of the implication relation is $Q \to_w t$, meaning that the term t is implied by Q to a certain degree w. Such a degree or weight can be easily incorporated into a retrieval model. The same expression can be used for cross-language implication relations with terms in a different language.

This unified view has been advocated in Nie (2003). The above comparision clearly shows that there is a strong parallel between query expansion and query translation. This suggests a possible look into the future of query expansion in CLIR as a process strongly inspired by query expansion, which has a long history in IR.

5.2.2 Inspiring Query Translation from Query Expansion—An Example

Given the strong similarity we established one can naturally ask the question: what query expansion approaches can be adapted to query translation? To this question, our general answer is: virtually any query expansion approach could be adapted to query expansion. In this section, we describe one recent query expansion approach—context-dependent query expansion, and discuss how it could be adapted to CLIR.

Query expansion using co-occurrences typically tries to extract relations between terms and use them to expand queries. Notice that in most cases, the extracted relations between terms are context-independent, i.e., no context information is specified in such a relation. Most often relations are set up from a single term to another, such as "program $\to_w$ computer." A drawback often observed is that such relations are ambiguous. Indeed, the term "program" may, or may not, be related to "computer" depending on its context of utilization. Using such a relation regardless of context will generate a great amount of noise.

Attempts have been made to incorporate some query context into consideration during query expansion. The idea is to be able to use additional contextual information from the query to help select more appropriate expansion terms. Qiu and Frei (1993) is an example of context-dependent query expansion. It selects expansion terms according to their global similarity to all the query terms (formulated as a sum). As a result, a candidate expansion term related to more initial query terms is preferred. This is an indirect way to account for context. A more direct way is to incorporate some context term in the relations themselves (Bai et al., 2007): the traditional co-occurrence relation between two single terms is extended to consider more than one term in the condition part. For example, rather than determining expansion terms t such that "insider $\rightarrow t$" and "trading $\rightarrow t$," one can determine the relation "(insider, trading) $\rightarrow t$," meaning that t is implied in the context of observing both "insider" and "trading." The combination "(insider, trading)" forms a stronger context than a single term "insider" or "trading." This is the reason why the approach is called context-dependent query expansion. For a query "insider trading," the latter relation can suggest expansion terms much more strongly related to it than the former relations. For example, strongly related terms such as "fraud," "Boesky," and "Drexel" (a company involved in an insider trading scandal) have been identified for this query, while the context-independent relations also suggest less strongly related terms such as "exchange," considered to be related to "trading." The experiments reported in Bai et al. (2007) have proven the approach to be more effective than previous context-independent expansion approaches. We can see here that the use of stronger context is highly beneficial in query expansion.

The question now is: can we use a similar method in query translation? A similar approach would mean that, instead of estimating translation probability $P(t_2|t_1)$ between a pair of single words, we estimate $P(t_3|t_1, t_2)$ (if the condition part is limited to two terms). For example, instead of estimating $P(t|\text{drug})$ and $P(t|\text{traffic})$ for a possible translation term t, we estimate $P(t|\text{drug, traffic})$. If we still rely on parallel sentences to estimate the latter probability, we will require that t co-occurs strongly with both "drug" and "traffic" in the aligned sentences. Such an approach would enable us to determine more appropriate translation terms and help solve translation ambiguities.

One may notice that the suggested approach goes in the same direction as phrase-based MT (Kohen et al., 2003), which translate a phrase (a consecutive sequence of words) together as a unit. However, as we already discussed, query translation in CLIR can be significantly different from SMT: the context word useful for the selection of translation can be a word that is not adjacent to the give word. It could be a co-occuring word at some distance. So, one cannot directly use phrase-based translation model in SMT. Instead, a specific translation model should be developed. In addition, the goal of translation in CLIR is not merely to produce a literal translation, but to produce useful terms allowing us to retrieve relevant documents. This implies that the strict phrase translation relations should be extended significantly to encompass related terms useful for CLIR.

The above description points to some possible avenues for future developments of context-dependent query translation in CLIR.

(1) One can directly adapt the method proposed in Bai et al. (2007) to estimate cross-language term similarity that is more context-dependent.

(2) One can also modify the model training process in SMT to incorporate more flexible "phrases," not limited to consecutive words. This higher flexibility will greatly increase the complexity: virtually any pair of words in a source-language sentence can form such a "phrase." In order to reduce complexity, it will be necessary to perform some selection of the "phrases" to be kept. Different criteria can be used for this: mutual information, syntactic structure, distance, etc. The selection can also be done before the training process or within the training process.

(3) The training process of a translation model for CLIR can have the specific goal of maximizing the CLIR effectiveness (e.g., MAP). Translation models in SMT are trained for a related, but different goal—the generation of the aligned target language sentence. The goal of a translation model for CLIR should not be limited to this and should take into account the other aspects of CLIR.

Our description is not aimed to advocate the above specific approaches for query translation. It is rather an example to show that by inspiring from query expansion in monolingual IR, more doors are open for CLIR. There are many more promising avenues and interesting problems for future research and development in CLIR that can inspire from query expansion and other approaches developed in monolingual IR. What we advocate here is to have a broader view of CLIR than just translation. Translation is part of CLIR, as query expansion is in monolingual IR. We believe that this broader view of CLIR could enable us to develop new approaches by inspiring from monolingual IR.

·   ·   ·   ·

References

AbdulJaleel, N., and Larkey, L. S. (2003). "Statistical transliteration for English-Arabic cross-language information retrieval," in *Proceedings of CIKM Conference*, pp. 139–146.

Adriani, M., and van Rijsbergen, C. J. (2000). "Phrase identification in cross-language information retrieval," in *Proceedings of RIAO Conference*, pp. 520–528.

Adriani, M., and Wahyu, I. (2005). "The performance of a machine translation-based English-Indonesian CLIR System," in *Proceedings of CLEF Conference*, pp. 151–154. doi:10.1007/11878773_16

Alfonseca, E., Bilac, S., and Pharies, S. (2008). "Decompounding query keywords from compounding languages," in *Proceedings of ACL-HLT Conference*, pp. 253–256. doi:10.3115/1557690.1557763

Baeza-Yates, R., and Ribeiro-Neto, B. (1999). *Modern Information Retrieval*: Addison Wesley Press.

Bai, J., Nie, J.-Y., Bouchard, H., and Cao, G. (2007). "Using query contexts in information retrieval," in *Proceedings of SIGIR Conference*, pp. 15–22. doi:10.1145/1277741.1277747

Bai, J., Song, D., Bruza, P., Nie, J.-Y., and Cao, G. (2005). "Query expansion using term relationships in language models for information retrieval," in *Proceedings of CIKM Conference*, pp. 688–695. doi:10.1145/1099554.1099725

Ballesteros, L., and Croft, W. B. (1997). "Phrasal translation and query expansion techniques for cross-language information retrieval," in *Proceedings of SIGIR Conference*, pp. 84-91. doi:10.1145/258525.258540

Ballesteros, L., and Croft, W. B. (1998). "Resolving ambiguity for cross-language retrieval," in *Proceedings of SIGIR Conference*, pp. 64–71. doi:10.1145/290941.290958

Berger, A., and Lafferty, J. (1999). "Information retrieval as statistical translation," in *Proceedings of SIGIR Conference*, pp. 222–229. doi:10.1145/312624.312681

Braschler, M., and Ripplinger, B. (2004). "How effective is stemming and decompounding for German Text Retrieval?" *Information Retrieval*, 7(3-4), pp. 291–316. doi:10.1023/B:INRT.0000011208.60754.a1

Braschler, M., and Schäuble, P. (2000). "Using corpus-based approaches in a system for multilingual information retrieval," *Information Retrieval*, 3(3), pp. 273–284.

Braschler, M., and Schäuble, P. (2001). "Experiments with the Eurospider retrieval system for CLEF 2000," in *Proceedings of CLEF Conference*, pp. 140–148. doi:10.1007/3-540-44645-1_13

Brin, S., and Page, L. (1998). "The anatomy of a large-scale hypertextual Web search engine," *WWW7/Computer Networks and ISDN Systems*, 20, pp. 107–117. doi:10.1016/S0169-7552(98)00110-X

Broglio, J., Callan, J. P., and Croft, W. B. (1994). "INQUERY system overview," in *Proceedings of TIPSTER Text Program (Phase I)*, pp. 47–67.

Brown, P., Della Pietra, S., Della Pietra, V., and Mercer, R. (1993). "The mathematics of statistical machine translation: parameter estimation," *Computational Linguistics*, 19(2), pp. 263–311.

Brown, P., Lai, J., and Mercer, R. (1991). "Aligning sentences in parallel corpora," in *Proceedings of ACL Conference*, pp. 169–176. doi:10.3115/981344.981366

Buckley, C., Mitra, M., Walz, J., and Cardie, C. (2000). "Using clustering and superconcepts within SMART: TREC 6," *Information Processing and Management*, 36(1), pp. 109–131. doi:10.1016/S0306-4573(99)00047-3

Cao, G., Gao, J., and Nie, J.-Y. (2007a). "Extending query translation to cross-language query expansion with Markov chain models," in *Proceedings of CIKM Conference*, pp. 351–360. doi:10.1145/1321440.1321491

Cao, G., Gao, J., and Nie, J.-Y. (2007b). "A system to mine large-scale bilingual dictionaries from monolingual Web pages," in *Proceedings of MT Summit Conference*, pp. 57–64.

Cao, G., Nie, J.-Y., and Bai, J. (2005). "Integrating word relationships into language modeling," in *Proceedings of SIGIR Conference*, pp. 298–305.

Carbonell, J. G., Yang, Y., Frederking, R. E., Brown, R. D., and Geng, Y., Lee, D. (1997). "Translingual information retrieval," in *Proceedings of IJCAI Conference*, pp. 708–714.

Chen, A., and Gey, F. C. (2001). "Translation term weighting and combining translation resources in cross-language retrieval," in *Proceedings of TREC Conference*.

Chen, A., and Gey, F. C. (2002). "Building an Arabic stemmer for information retrieval," in *Proceedings of TREC Conference*, pp. 631–639.

Chen, A., and Gey, F. C. (2003). "Experiments on cross-language and patent retrieval at NTCIR-3," in *Proceedings of NTCIR Workshop*.

Chen, A., He, J., Xu, L., Gey, F. C., and Meggs, J. (1997). "Chinese text retrieval without using a dictionary," in *Proceedings of SIGIR Conference*, pp. 42–49. doi:10.1145/258525.258532

Chen, A., Jiang, H., and Gey, F. C. (2000). "Combining multiple sources for short query translation in Chinese-English cross-language information retrieval," in *Proceedings of Workshop on information Retrieval with Asian Languages (IRAL)*, pp. 17–23. doi:10.1145/355214.355217

Chen, H. H., Lin, W. C., and Yang, C. H. (2006). "Translation-transliterating named entities for multilingual information access," *Journal of the American Society for Information Science and Technology*, 57(5), pp. 645–659. doi:10.1002/asi.20327

Chen, J., and Nie, J.-Y. (2000). "Automatic construction of parallel English-Chinese corpus for cross-language information retrieval," in *Proceedings of NAACL-ANLP Conference*, pp. 21–28.

Cheng, P., Teng, J., Chen, R., Wang, J., Lu, W., and Chien, L. (2004). "Translating unknown queries with Web corpora for cross-language information retrieval," in *Proceedings of SIGIR Conference*, pp. 162–169. doi:10.1145/1008992.1009020

Crouch, C. J., and Yang, B. (1992). "Experiments in automatic statistical thesaurus construction," in *Proceedings of SIGIR Conference*, pp. 77–88. doi:10.1145/133160.133180

Darwish, K., and Oard, D. W. (2002). "CLIR experiments at Maryland for TREC-2002: Evidence combination for Arabic-English retrieval," in *Proceedings of TREC Conference*.

Davis, M., and Dunning, T. (1995). "A TREC evaluation of query translation methods for multilingual text retrieval," in *Proceedings of TREC Conference*, pp. 483–497.

Davis, M. W., and Ogden, W. C. (1997). "Free resources and advanced alignment for cross-language text retrieval," in *Proceedings of TREC Conference*.

Deerwester, S., Dumais, S. T., Furnas, G. W., Landauer, T. K., and Harshman, R. (1990). "Indexing by Latent Semantic Analysis," *Journal of the Society for Information Science*, 41(6), pp. 391–407. doi:10.1002/(SICI)1097-4571(199009)41:6<391::AID-ASI1>3.0.CO;2-9

Dempster, A., Laird, N., and Rubin, D. (1977). "Maximum likelihood from incomplete data via the EM algorithm," *Journal of the Royal Statistical Society, Series B*, 39(1), pp. 1–38.

Dolamic, L., and Savoy, J. (2007). "Stemming approaches for East European languages," in *Proceedings of CLEF Conference*, pp. 37–44.

Dorr, B., Hovy, E., and Levin, L. (2004). "Machine Translation: Interlingual Methods," in K. Brown, (ed.), *Encyclopedia of Language and Linguistics, 2nd edition ms. 939*.

Dumais, S. T. (1994). "Latent Semantic Indexing (LSI) and TREC-2," in *Proceedings of TREC Conference*, pp. 105–116.

Dumais, S. T., Landauer, T. K., and Littman, M. L. (1996). "Automatic cross-linguistic information retrieval using Latent Semantic Indexing," in *Proceedings of SIGIR Workshop on Cross-Linguistic Information Retrieval*, pp. 16–23.

Dumais, S. T., Letsche, T. A., Littman, M. L., and Landauer, T. K. (1997). "Automatic cross-language retrieval using Latent Semantic Indexing," in *Proceedings of AAAI Spring Symposium on Cross-Language Text and Speech Retrieval*.

Federico, M., and Bertoldi, N. (2002). "Statistical cross-language information retrieval using n-best query translations," in *Proceedings of SIGIR Conference*, pp. 167–174. doi:10.1145/564376.564407

Franz, M., McCarley, J. S., and Roukos, S. (1999). "Ad hoc and multilingual information retrieval at IBM," in *Proceedings of TREC Conference*.

Fuhr, N. (1992). "Probabilistic Models in Information Retrieval," *Computer Journal*, 35(3), pp. 243–255. doi:10.1093/comjnl/35.3.243

Gale, W. A., and Church, K. W. (1993). "A program for aligning sentences in bilingual corpora," *Computational Linguistics*, 19(3), pp. 75–102.

Gao, J., Goodman, J., Cao, G., and Li, H. (2002). "Exploring asymmetric clustering for statistical language modeling," in *Proceedings of ACL Conference*, pp. 465–472.

Gao, J., Nie, J.-Y., Wu, G., and Cao, G. (2004a). "Dependence language model for information retrieval," in *Proceedings of SIGIR Conference*, pp. 170–177. doi:10.1145/1008992.1009024

Gao, J., and Nie, J.-Y. (2006). "A study of statistical models for query translation: Find a good unit of translation," in *Proceedings of SIGIR Conference*, pp. 194–201.

Gao, J., Nie, J.-Y., Xun, E., Zhang, J., Zhou, M., and Huang, C. (2001). "Improving query translation for cross-language information retrieval using statistical models," in *Proceedings of SIGIR Conference*, pp. 96–104. doi:10.1145/383952.383966

Gao, W., Wong, K. F., and Lam, W. (2004b). "Phoneme-based transliteration of foreign names in cross language information retrieval," in *Proceedings of IJCNLP Conference*, pp. 374–381.

Gey, F., Jiang, H., Chen, A., and Larson, R. R. (1999). "Manual queries and machine translation in cross-language retrieval and interactive retrieval with Cheshire II at TREC-7," in *Proceedings of TREC Conference*, pp. 527–540.

Gey, F. C., and Jiang, H. (2000). "English–German cross-language retrieval for the GIRT collection—exploiting a multilingual thesaurus," in *Proceedings of TREC Conference*, pp. 301–306.

Gilarranz, J., Ginzalo, J., and Verdejo, F. (1996). "An approach to conceptual text retrieval using the EuroWordnet multilingual semantic database," in *Proceedings of AAAI-96 Spring Symposium on Cross-Language Text and Speech Retrieval*.

Gollins, T., and Sanderson, M. (2001). "Improving cross language retrieval with triangulated translation," in *Proceedings of SIGIR Conference*, pp. 90–95. doi:10.1145/383952.383965

Grefenstette, G. (1999). "The World Wide Web as a resource for example-based machine translation tasks," in *Proceedings of ASLIB translating and the computer 21 conference*.

Harman, D. (1994). "Overview of the Second Text REtrieval Conference (TREC-2)," in *Proceedings of TREC Conference*, pp. 1–20. doi:10.3115/1075812.1075894

Hedlund, T., Keskustalo, H., Pirkola, A., Airio, E., and Järvelin, K. (2001). "Utaclir @ CLEF 2001—effects of compound splitting and n-gram techniques," in *Proceedings of CLEF Conference*, pp. 118–136.

Hiemstra, D., and Kraaij, W. (1998). "Twenty-one at TREC-7: ad-hoc and cross-language track," in *Proceedings of TREC Conference*.

Hildebrand, A. S., Eck, M., Vogel, S., and Waibel, A. (2005). "Adaptation of the translation model for statistical machine translation based on information retrieval," in *Proceedings of EAMT Conference*, pp. 133–142.

Huang, F., Zhang, Y., and Vogel, S. (2005). "Mining key phrase translations from Web corpora," in *Proceedings of HLT-EMNLP Conference*, pp. 483–490. doi:10.3115/1220575.1220636

Huang, S., and Tilley, S. (2001). "Issues of content and structure for a multilingual web site," in *Proceedings of the 19th Annual international Conference on Computer Documentation*, pp. 103–110. doi:10.1145/501516.501537

Hull, D., and Grefenstette, G. (1996). "Querying across languages: A dictionary-based approach to multilingual information retrieval," in *Proceedings of SIGIR Conference*, pp. 49–57.

Hutchins, J. (1986). *Machine Translation: past, present, future*, Chichester: Ellis Horwood.

Hutchins, W. J., and Somers, H. L. (1992). *An Introduction to Machine Translation*: Academic Press.

Jagarlamudi, J., and Kumaran, A. (2007). "Cross-lingual information retrieval for system for Indian languages," in *Proceedings of CLEF Conference*, pp. 80–87.

Jang, M.-G., Myaeng, S. H., and Park, S. Y. (1999). "Using mutual information to resolve query translation ambiguities and query term weighting," in *Proceedings of ACL Conference*, pp. 223–229. doi:10.3115/1034678.1034718

Järvelin, K., and Kekalainen, J. (2002). "Cumulated gain-based evaluation of IR techniques," *ACM Transactions on Information Systems*, 20, pp. 422–446. doi:10.1145/582415.582418

Jelinek, F. (1998). *Statistical Methods for Speech Recognition*, Cambridge, MA: MIT Press.

Jones, G., Fantino, F., Newman, E., and Zhang, Y. (2008). "Domain-specific query translation for multilingual information access using machine translation augmented with dictionaries mined from Wikipedia," in *Proceedings of Workshop on Cross Lingual Information Access*, pp. 34–41.

Jones, G. J. F., Zhang, Y., Newman, E., Fantino, F., and Debole, F. (2007). "Multilingual search for cultural heritage archives via combining multiple translation resources," in *Proceedings of LaTeCH 2007—ACL Workshop on Language Technology for Cultural Heritage Data*.

Kadri, Y., and Nie, J. Y. (2006). "Effective stemming for Arabic information retrieval," in *Proceedings of The Challenge of Arabic for NLP/MT, International Conf. at the British Computer Society (BCS)*, pp. 68–74.

Kang, B.-J., and Choi, K.-S. (2000). "Two approaches for the resolution of word mismatch problem caused by English words and foreign words in Korean information retrieval," in *Proceedings of the Fifth International Workshop on Information Retrieval with Asian Languages*, pp. 133–140. doi:10.1145/355214.355234

Kay, M., and Röscheisen, M. (1988). *Text-Translation Alignment*. Xerox Palo Alto Research Center.

Kishida, K., and Kando, N. (2005). "Hybrid approach of query and document translation with pivot language for cross-language information retrieval," in *Proceedings of CLEF Conference*.

Knight, K. (1999). "A Statistical MT Tutorial Workbook." http://www.isi.edu/natural-language/mt/wkbm.rtf.

Knight, K., and Graehl, J. (1998). "Machine transliteration," *Computational Linguistics*, 24(4), pp. 599–612.

Kohen, P., Och, F. J., and Marcus, D. (2003). "Statistical phrase-based translation," in *Proceedings of HLT-NAACL Conference*, pp. 48–54. doi:10.3115/1073445.1073462

Kraaij, W., Nie, J.-Y., and Simard, M. (2003). "Embedding Web-based statistical translation models in cross-language information retrieval," *Computational Linguistics*, 29(3), pp. 381–420. doi:10.1162/089120103322711587

Kraft, D. H., and Buell, D. A. (1983). "Fuzzy sets and generalized Boolean retrieval systems." *International Journal on Man-Machine Studies*, 19, pp. 49–56. doi:10.1016/S0020-7373(83)80041-8

Krovetz, R. (1993). "Viewing morphology as an inference process," in *Proceedings of SIGIR Conference*, pp. 191–202. doi:10.1145/160688.160718

Kuo, J. S., Li, H., and Yang, Y. K. (2006). "Learning transliteration lexicon from the Web," in *Proceedings of COLING-ACL Conference*, pp. 1129–1136. doi:10.3115/1220175.1220317

Kwok, K. L. (1999). "English–Chinese cross-language retrieval based on a translation package," in *Proceedings of Workshop of Machine Translation for Cross Language Information Retrieval, Machine Translation Summit VII*.

Kwok, K. L., and Grunfeld, L. (1996). "TREC-5 English and Chinese retrieval experiments using PIRCS," in *Proceedings of TREC Conference*.

Larkey, L. S., Ballesteros, L., and Connell, M. E. (2002). "Improving stemming for Arabic information retrieval: light stemming and co-occurrence analysis," in *Proceedings of SIGIR Conference*, pp. 275–282.

Lavrenko, V., Choquette, M., and Croft, W. B. (2002). "Cross-lingual relevance models," in *Proceedings of SIGIR Conference*, pp. 175–182. doi:10.1145/564376.564408

Lavrenko, V., and Croft, W. B. (2001). "Relevance-based language models," in *Proceedings of SIGIR Conference*, pp. 120–127. doi:10.1145/383952.383972

Lee, J. H., Cho, H. Y., and Park, H. O. (1999). "N-gram-based indexing for Korean text retrieval." *Information Processing and Management*, 35(4), pp. 427–441. doi:10.1016/S0306-4573(98)00050-8

Lehtokangas, R., Airio, E., and Järvelin, K. (2004). "Transitive dictionary translation challenges direct dictionary translation in CLIR." *Information Processing and Management*, 40(6), pp. 973–988.

Lesk, M. (1986). "Automatic sense disambiguation using machine readable dictionaries: how to tell a pine cone from an ice cream cone." *The 5th annual international conference on Systems documentation*.

Levow, G.-A., Oard, D. W., and Resnik, P. (2005). "Dictionary-based techniques for cross-language information retrieval," *Information Processing and Management*, 41, pp. 523–547.

Li, Q., Chen, Y. P., Myaeng, S.-H., Jin, Y., and Kang, B.-Y. (2009). "Concept unification of terms in different languages via Web mining for information retrieval," *Information Processing and Management*, 45(2), pp. 246–262.

Lin, W. C., and Chen, H. H. (2003). "Description of NTU approach to NTCIR3 multilingual information retrieval," in *Proceedings of the Third NTCIR workshop*.

Liu, T.-Y. (2009). "Learning to rank for information retrieval." *Foundations and Trends in Information Retrieval*, 3(3), pp. 225–331.

Liu, Y., Jin, R., and Chai, J. Y. (2005). "A maximum coherence model for dictionary-based cross-language information retrieval," in *Proceedings of SIGIR Conference*, pp. 536–543.

López-Ostenero, F., Gonzalo, J., and Verdejo, F. (2005). "Noun phrases as building blocks for cross-language search assistance," *Information Processing and Management*, 41(3), pp. 549–568.

Lu, W., Chien, L. F., and Lee, H. (2004). "Anchor text mining for translation of Web queries: a transitive translation approach." *ACM Transactions on Information Systems*, 22, pp. 242–269.

Maeda, A., Sadat, F., Yoshikawa, M., and Uemura, S. (2000). "Query term disambiguation for web cross-language information retrieval using a search engine," in *Proceedings of the 5th International Workshop on Information Retrieval with Asian Languages (IRAL)*, pp. 25–32. doi:10.1145/355214.355218

Mandala, R., Tokunaga, T., and Tanaka, H. (1998). "Ad hoc retrieval erxperiments using WordNet and automatically constructed thesauri," in *Proceedings of TREC Conference*, pp. 475–481.

Manning, C., Raghavan, P., and Schütze, H. (2008). *Introduction to Information Retrieval*: Cambridge University Press.

Manning, C., and Schütze, H. (1999). *Foundations of statistical Natural Language Processing*. Cambridge, MA: MIT Press.

McCarley, J. S. (1999). "Should we translate the documents or the queries in cross-language information retrieval," in *Proceedings of ACL Conference*, pp. 208–214. doi:10.3115/1034678.1034716

McNamee, P., and Mayfield, J. (2002). "Comparing cross-language query expansion techniques by degrading translation resources," in *Proceedings of SIGIR Conference*, pp. 159–166. doi:10.1145/564376.564406

McNamee, P., and Mayfield, J. (2004a). "Character N-gram tokenization for European language text retrieval," *Information Retrieval*, 7(1–2), pp. 73–97. doi:10.1023/B:INRT.0000009441.78971.be

McNamee, P., and Mayfield, J. (2004b). "Cross-language retrieval using HAIRCUT at CLEF 2004," in *Proceedings of CLEF Conference*.

Meng, H., Chen, B., Grams, E., Lo, W.-K., Levow, G.-A., Oard, D., Schone, P., Tang, K., and Wang, J. Q. (2001). "Mandarin–English information (MEI): investigating translingual speech retrieval," in *Proceedings of Human Language Technology (HLT) Conference*, pp. 239–245.

Metzler, D., and Croft, W. B. (2005). "A Markov random field model for term dependencies," in *Proceedings of SIGIR Conference*, pp. 472–479. doi:10.1145/1076034.1076115

Miller, D., Leek, T., and Schwartz, R. (1999). "A hidden Markov model information retrieval system," in *Proceedings of SIGIR Conference*, pp. 214–222. doi:10.1145/312624.312680

Miller, G. A. (1995). "WordNet: a lexical database for English," *Communications of the ACM*, 38(11), pp. 39–41. doi:10.1145/219717.219748

Monz, C., and Dorr, B. (2005). "Iterative translation disambiguation for cross-language information retrieval," in *Proceedings of SIGIR Conference*, pp. 520–527. doi:10.1145/1076034.1076123

Moreau, F., Claveau, V., and Sébillot, P. (2007). "Automatic morphological query expansion using analogy-based machine learning," in *Proceedings of ECIR Conference*, pp. 222–233. doi:10.1007/978-3-540-71496-5_22

Mori, T., Kokubu, T., and Tanaka, T. (2001). "Cross-lingual information retrieval based on LSI with multiple word spaces," in *Proceedings of NTCIR Workshop*.

Moulinier, I., and Molina-Salgado, H. (2003). "Thomson legal and regulatory experiments for CLEF 2002," in *Proceedings of CLEF, LNCS 2785*, pp. 155–163.

Nagata, M., Saito, T., and Suzuki, K. (2001). "Using the Web as a bilingual dictionary," in *Proceedings of the Workshop on Data-Driven Methods in Machine Translation (held with ACL Conf.)*, pp. 1–8. doi:10.3115/1118037.1118050

Nie, J.-Y. (2003). "Query expansion and query translation as logical inference." *Journal of the American Society for Information Science and Technology*, 54(4), pp. 335–346. doi:10.1002/asi.10214

Nie, J.-Y., Isabelle, P., Plamondon, P., and Foster, G. (1998). "Using a probabilistic translation model for cross-language information retrieval," in *Proceedings of Sixth Workshop on Very Large Corpora*.

Nie, J.-Y., and Ren, F. (1999). "Chinese information retrieval: using characters or words?" *Information Processing and Management*, 35, pp. 443–462. doi:10.1016/S0306-4573(98)00051-X

Nie, J.-Y., and Simard, M. (2001). "Using Statistical Translation Models for Bilingual IR," in *Proceedings of CLEF Conference*.

Nie, J.-Y., Simard, M., Isabelle, P., and Durand, R. (1999). "Cross-Language Information Retrieval based on Parallel Texts and Automatic Mining of Parallel Texts in the Web," in *Proceedings of SIGIR Conference*, pp. 74–81. doi:10.1145/312624.312656

Oard, D. and Dorr, B. (1996). *A survey of multilingual text retrieval*. University of Maryland, UMIACS-TR-96-19 CS-TR-3615.

Oard, D., W., He, D., and Wang, J. (2008). "User-assisted query translation for interactive cross-language information retrieval," *Information Processing and Management*, 44(1), pp. 181–211. doi:10.1016/j.ipm.2006.12.009

Oard, D. W., Gonzalo, J., Sanderson, M., López-Ostenero, F., and Wang, J. (2004). "Interactive cross-language document selection," *Information Retrieval*, 7(1–2), pp. 205–228. doi:10.1023/B:INRT.0000009446.22036.e3

Oard, D. W., and Hackett, P. (1997). "Document Translation for the Cross-Language Text Retrieval at the University of Maryland," in *Proceedings of TREC Conference*.

Och, F. J., and Ney, H. (2003). "A systematic comparison of various statistical alignment models," *Computational Linguistics*, 29(1), pp. 19–51. doi:10.1162/089120103321337421

Ogawa, Y., and Matsuda, T. (1999). "Overlapping statistical segmentation for effective indexing of Japanese text," *Information Processing and Management*, 35(4), pp. 465–480. doi:10.1016/S0306-4573(98)00052-1

Papineni, K., Roukos, S., Ward, T., and Zhu, W.-J. (2001). *BLEU: a method for automatic evaluation of machine translation*. IBM Research RC22176 (W0109-022).

Peng, F., Feng, F., and McCallum, A. (2004). "Chinese segmentation and new word detection using conditional random fields," in *Proceedings of ACL Conference*, pp. 562–568. doi:10.3115/1220355.1220436

Pirkola, A. (1998). "The effects of query structure and dictionary setups in dictionary-based cross-language information retrieval," in *Proceedings of SIGIR Conference*, pp. 55–63.

Pirkola, A., Toivonen, J., Keskustalo, H., and Järvelin, K. (2007). "Frequency-based identification of correct translation equivalent (FITE) obtained through transformation rules." *ACM Transactions on Information Systems*, 26(1). doi:10.1145/1292591.1292593

Pirkola, A., Toivonen, J., Keskustalo, H., Visala, K., and Järvelin, K. (2003). "Fuzzy translation of cross-lingual spelling variants," in *Proceedings of SIGIR Conference*, pp. 45–352. doi:10.1145/860435.860498

Ponte, J., and Croft, W. B. (1998). "A language modeling approach to information retrieval," in *Proceedings of SIGIR Conference*, pp. 275–281. doi:10.1145/290941.291008

Porter, M. (1980). "An algorithm for suffix stripping," *Program*, 14(3), pp. 130–137. doi:10.1108/eb046814

Qiu, Y., and Frei, H. P. (1993). "Concept query expansion," in *Proceedings of SIGIR Conference*, pp. 160–169. doi:10.1145/160688.160713

Qu, Y., Grefenstette, G., and Evans, D. A. (2003). "Automatic transliteration for Japanese-to-English text retrieval," in *Proceedings of SIGIR Conference*, pp. 353–360. doi:10.1145/860435.860499

Radecki, T. (1979). "Fuzzy set theoretical approach to document retrieval," *Information Processing and Management*, 15, pp. 247–259. doi:10.1016/0306-4573(79)90031-1

Resnik, P. (1998). "Parallel Strands: A preliminary investigation into mining the Web for bilingual text," in *Proceedings of AMTA Conference*, pp. 72–82. doi:10.1007/3-540-49478-2_7

Resnik, P., and Smith, N. A. (2003). "The Web as a parallel corpus," *Computational Linguistics*, 29(3), pp. 349–380. doi:10.1162/089120103322711578

Robertson, S., and Spärck Jones, K. (1976). "Relevance weighting of search terms," *Journal of the American Society for Information Science*, 27, pp. 129–146. doi:10.1002/asi.4630270302

Ruiz, M., Diekema, A., and Sheridan, P. (2000). "CINDOR Conceptual Interlingua Document Retrieval: TREC-8 Evaluation," in *Proceedings of TREC Conference*.

Salton, G. (1970). "Automatic processing of foreign language documents." *Journal of the American Society for Information Science*, 21(3), pp. 187–194. doi:10.1002/asi.4630210305

Salton, G., Fox, E. A., and Wu, H. (1983). "Extended Boolean information retrieval," *Communications of the ACM*, 26(12), pp. 1022–1036.

Salton, G., and McGill, M. (1983). *Introduction to Modern Information Retrieval*. McGraw-Hill. doi:10.1145/182.358466

Salton, G., Wong, A., and Yang, C. S. (1975). "A vector space model for automatic indexing," *Communications of the ACM*, 18(11), pp. 613–620. doi:10.1145/361219.361220

Savoy, J. (1993). "Stemming of French words based on grammatical categories," *Journal of the American Society for Information Science*, 44(1), pp. 1–9. doi:10.1002/(SICI)1097-4571(199301)44:1<1:: AID-ASI1>3.0.CO;2-1

Savoy, J. (1999). "A stemming procedure and stopword list for general french corpora," *Journal of the American Society for Information Science*, 50(10), pp. 944–952. doi:10.1002/(SICI)1097-4571(1999)50:10<944::AID-ASI9>3.0.CO;2-Q

Savoy, J. (2006). "Light stemming approaches for the French, Portuguese, German and Hungarian languages," in *Proceedings of ACM SAC Conference*, pp. 1031–1035. doi:10.1145/1141277.1141523

Savoy, J. (2007). "Searching strategies for the Bulgarian language," *Information Retrieval*, 10(6), pp. 509–529. doi:10.1007/s10791-007-9033-9

Schäuble, P., and Sheridan, P. (1997). "Cross-language information retrieval (CLIR) track overview," in *Proceedings of TREC Conference*, pp. 31–44.

Schönhofen, P., Benczúr, A., Bíró, I., and Csalogány, K. (2007). "Performing cross-language retrieval with Wikipedia," in *Proceedings of CLEF Conference*.

Seo, H.-C., Kim, S.-B., Rim, H.-C., and Myaeng, S.-H. (2005). "Improving query translation in English–Korean cross-language information retrieval," *Information Processing and Management*, 41, pp. 507–522. doi:10.1016/j.ipm.2004.06.011

Sheridan, P., and Ballerini, J. P. (1996). "Experiments in multilingual information retrieval using the SPIDER system," in *Proceedings of SIGIR Conference*, pp. 58–65. doi:10.1145/243199.243213

Shi, L., Nie, J. Y., and Bai, J. (2007). "Comparing different units for query translation for Chinese cross-language information retrieval," in *Proceedings of Infoscale Conference*.

Simard, M., Foster, G., and Isabelle, P. (1992). "Using cognates to align sentences in bilingual corpora," in *Proceedings of TMI Conference*.

Šnajder, J., Dalbelo Bašić, B., and Tadić, M. (2008). "Automatic acquisition of inflectional lexica for morphological normalization," *Information Processing and Management*, 44(5), pp. 1720–1731.

Song, F., and Croft, W. B. (1999). "A general language model for information retrieval," in *Proceedings of SIGIR Conference*, pp. 279–280. doi:10.1145/312624.312698

Sproat, R., and Emerson, T. (2003). "The first international Chinese word segmentation bakeoff," in *Proceedings of SIGHAN Workshop On Chinese Language Processing*. doi:10.3115/1119250.1119269

Tomlinson, S. (2004). "Experiments with decompounded Chinese, Japanese and Korean words parsed by Hammingbird SearchServer," in *Proceedings of NTCIR Workshop*.

Van Rijsbergen, C. J. (1979). *Information retrieval*. London: Butterworths. doi:10.1016/S0003-2670(01)83552-2

Vauquois, B. (1968). "A survey of formal grammars and algorithms for recognition and transformation in machine translation," in *Proceedings of IFIP Congress-6*, pp. 254–260.

Voorhees, E. M. (1993). "Using WordNet to disambiguate word senses for text retrieval," in *Proceedings of SIGIR Conference*, pp. 171–180. doi:10.1145/160688.160715

Voorhees, E. M. (1994). "Query expansion using lexical-semantic relations," in *Proceedings of SIGIR Conference*, pp. 61–69.

Voorhees, E. M., and Harman, D. (1997). "Overview of the Sixth Text Retrieval Conference (TREC-6)," in *Proceedings of TREC Conference*, pp. 1–24.

Wan, S., and Verspoor C. (1998). "Automatic English-Chinese name transliteration for development of multilingual resources," *Proceedings of the International Conference on Computational Linguistics (COLING)*, pp. 1352–1356. doi:10.3115/980432.980789

Wang, J., and Oard, D. (2006). "Combining bidirectional translation and synonymy for cross-language information retrieval," in *Proceedings of SIGIR Conference*, pp. 202–209.

Wong, K.-F., Li, W., Xu, R., and Zhang, Z.-S. (2009). *Introduction to Chinese Natural Language Processing*. Morgan & Claypool. doi:10.2200/S00211ED1V01Y200909HLT004

Wu, D. (1994). "Aligning a parallel English–Chinese corpus statistically with lexical criteria," in *Proceedings of ACL Conference*, pp. 80–87. doi:10.3115/981732.981744

Xu, J., and Croft, W. B. (1996). "Query expansion using local and global document analysis," in *Proceedings of SIGIR Conference*, pp. 4–11. doi:10.1145/243199.243202

Xu, J., Fraser, A., and Weischedel, R. (2002). "Empirical studies in strategies for Arabic retrieval," in *Proceedings of SIGIR Conference*, pp. 269–274. doi:10.1145/564376.564424

Xu, J., and Weischedel, R. (2000). "Cross-lingual information retrieval using hidden Markov models," in *Proceedings of SIGDAT Conference on Empirical Methods in Natural Language Processing and Very Large Corpora*, pp. 95–103. doi:10.3115/1117794.1117806

Xu, J., and Weischedel, R. (2005). "Empirical studies on the impact of lexical resources on CLIR performance," *Information Processing and Management*, 41, pp. 475–487. doi:10.1016/j.ipm.2004.06.009

Xu, J. X., Weischedel, R., and Nguyen, C. (2001). "Evaluating a probabilistic model for cross-lingual information retrieval," in *Proceedings of SIGIR Conference*, pp. 105–110.

Yang, Y., Carbonell, J. G., Brown, R. D., and Frederking, R. E. (1998). "Translingual information retrieval: learning from bilingual corpora," *Artificial Intelligence*, 103(1–2), pp. 323–345. doi:10.1016/S0004-3702(98)00063-0

Zhai, C., and Lafferty, J. (2001a). "Model-based feedback in the language modeling approach to information retrieval," in *Proceedings of CIKM Conference*, pp. 403–410. doi:10.1145/502585.502654

Zhai, C., and Lafferty, J. (2001b). "A study of smoothing methods for language models applied to information retrieval," in *Proceedings of SIGIR Conference*, pp. 334–342. doi:10.1145/383952.384019

Zhai, C. X. (2009). *Statistical Language Models for Information Retrieval.* Morgan & Claypool.

Zhang, H., Liu, Q., Cheng, X., Zhang, H., and Yu, H. (2003). "Chinese lexical analysis using hierarchical hidden Markov Model," in *Proceedings of Second SIGHAN Workshop*, pp. 63–70. doi:10.3115/1119250.1119259

Zhang, Y., Huang, F., and Vogel, S. (2005). "Mining translations of OOV terms from the Web through cross-lingual query expansion," in *Proceedings of SIGIR Conference*, pp. 669–670. doi:10.1145/1076034.1076182

Zhang, Y., and Vines, P. (2004). "Using the Web for automated translation extraction in cross-language information retrieval," in *Proceedings of SIGIR Conference*, pp. 162–169.

Zhou, D., Truran, M., Brailsford, T., and Ashman, H. (2008). "A hybrid technique for English–Chinese cross language information retrieval," *ACM Transactions on Asian Language Information Processing (TALIP)*, 7(2), pp. 1–35. doi:10.1145/1362782.1362784

Author Biography

Jian-Yun Nie is a professor at the Computer Science Department (Département d'Informatique et de Recherche Opérationnelle) in Université de Montréal. He obtained a Ph.D. in computer science (specialization in IR) in 1990 from Université Joseph Fourier of Grenoble, France, and a B.Ing. in computer science from the Institute of Technology of Nanjing (now Southeast University), China. His research has been focused on IR and NLP. Since his Ph.D. studies, he has worked on IR in different languages, CLIR, IR models, and statistical natural language analysis. He has published more than 150 research papers in these areas in journals and conferences. He has been a PC member of a large number of conferences. He will serve as a general co-chair of the ACM-SIGIR conference in 2011. He is currently on the editorial board of seven international journals. He has been an invited professor and researcher at several universities and companies.

Home page: http://www.iro.umontreal.ca/~nie/

Printed in the United States
by Baker & Taylor Publisher Services